ARDINIA

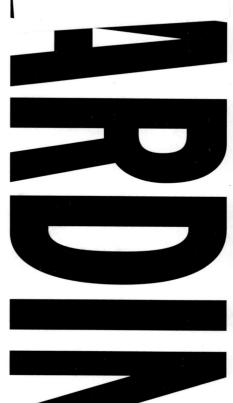

**SPIRAL**GUIDE

 Publishing

# Contents

Original text by Adele Evans
Revised and updated by Barbara and Stillman Rogers

Revision managed by Bookwork Creative Associates
Series Editor Karen Rigden
Series Designer Catherine Murray

Published by AA Publishing, a trading name of AA Media Limited,
whose registered office is Fanum House, Basing View, Basingstoke,
Hampshire, RG21 4EA. Registered number 06112600

ISBN: 978-0-7495-6814-6

We have tried to ensure accuracy in this guide, but things do
change, so please let us know if you have any comments at
travelguides@theAA.com

A CIP catalogue record for this book is available from the
British Library.

Cover design and binding style by permission of AA Publishing
Colour separation by AA Digital Department
Printed and bound in China by Leo Paper Products

Find out more about AA Publishing and the wide range of services
the AA provides by visiting our website at www.theAA.com/shop

A04413
Maps in this title produced from mapping © Freytag-Berndt u.
Artaria KG, 1231 Vienna-Austria

# The Magazine

A great holiday is more than just lying on a beach or shopping till you drop – to really get the most from your trip you need to know what makes the place tick. The Magazine provides an entertaining overview to some of the social, cultural and natural elements that make up the unique character of this engaging island.

# An Island with its
# Back to the Sea

**Cast away in the middle of the Mediterranean, the Italian island of Sardinia seems more like a small continent. The second largest island after Sicily, Sardinia has a coastline of almost 2,000km (1,240 miles) indented by tiny coves and guarded by towering cliffs.**

## Waves of Invaders

Inland you will find a traditional land of shepherds, of wild rolling hills and meadows bright with wildflowers – a place where it's very easy to forget that the sea is never far away.

Although Sardinia is an island, it is unlike one in many ways, and has always focused far more on its inland areas than on its shore. Traditional culture focuses on land and agriculture, and it has never been a place of seafarers or fishermen. For the Sardinians the sea has been synonymous with those who came to plunder, *"furat chi beit dae su mare"* ("he who comes from the sea comes to rob"). Phoenicians, Romans, Arabs, Catalans and mainland Italians all took – and left – their share.

This is not only key to understanding Sardinia, but it is what makes it especially interesting and surprising. Although unlike other islands in many ways, it is still quite insular, in spite of (actually, because of) its many invaders and influences.

**Tenutu Pilastre in Arzachena, an archetypical Sardinian village**

## THE SARD LANGUAGE

The Sard language is mostly based on Latin, but with smatterings surviving from the Nuraghic period, such as the word *nuraghe* itself. Other words bear Phoenician, Arabic, Corsican, Genoese, Catalan or other linguistic traces. Still widely spoken, and with countless different dialects, Sardinian coexists happily with Italian, which is spoken by just about everyone. But even on an island so small, there are clear regional linguistic differences, often based on the local invaders; in Alghero, for example, the Mass is still said in Catalan and signs are often in both Catalan and Italian.

## Self-Sufficiency

This insularity leads to its near fanaticism about local foods – Sardinians have always provided for themselves and protected what they had, instead of searching elsewhere for supplies. Even today they import a lot less food than most other islands. Sardinia's pastoral history has led to a thriving cheese industry as well as a wool industry that produced Italy's World War II uniform coats and still makes sought-after woven carpets.

## An Island Apart

The interest in land rather than sea shows in other ways: the trend towards agritourism lodgings (very popular here), the fascination with horses, the local handcrafts, the excellent wines, even the longevity of the people. Once you step beyond the dazzling beaches, this sharp contrast may be the first thing that strikes you. Explore further, and you will continue to marvel at how unusual Sardinia is, and how very insular it has remained in spite of its proximity to the mainland and its location in the middle of the Mediterranean sea routes.

This inland focus defines Sardinia and explains the roots of its culture, while touching on what makes it such an interesting place to visit.

# NURAGHI
## Giants' Tombs and Fairy Houses

**The more than 7,000 round stone towers rising up to 14m (45 feet) above the landscape would be interesting from any era, but when you realize that these were built between the 12th and 15th centuries BC, they become mind-boggling.**

### Feat of Engineering

Originally as tall as 18m (60 feet), *nuraghi* are built of huge stones that form walls and ceilings for as many as three interior floors. Built without mortar or any bonding substance, these walls have highly sophisticated inner staircases spiralling within their 2m (6 feet) thickness. How prehistoric people engineered these constructions remains a mystery.

Just as puzzling is their purpose and use. Archaeologists have found no evidence that they were used as living quarters, such as fires, food or household artefacts. Many *nuraghi* were surrounded by villages of stone round huts, but with wood and reed roofs instead of the stone *thalos* domes of

### BUILDING THE NURAGHI

When the towers were built about 3,500 years ago, the true dome, using a keystone, had not been invented. Nuraghic builders used instead an ancient method called a *thalos* dome to roof each level. With this method, each succeeding course of stone overhangs inward from the last until they meet at the top.

A higher storey can be added by laying a flat capstone over the top and filling in the edges to create a level floor.

the Nuraghic towers. These reveal ample evidence of household use, so it is surmised that the towers were built for observation, defence and as symbols of power to warn off potential invaders.

Whatever their purpose *nuraghi* are among the most interesting and amazing prehistoric relics in the world, and they are widespread enough that visitors to any part of the island can find one close by to explore.

## Supernatural Homes

It's easy to see how, millennia later, people came to view the mysterious graves left by their prehistoric forebears as supernatural places. Earth mound coverings of chambered tombs washed away and revealed what indeed look like tombs for giants, while little "rooms" carved into soft ledges and cliffs would make credible homes for wee folk. Archaeologists recognize these as group burial sites, and what little they know of the builders is gleaned from the bronze, pottery and stone offerings left with the deceased. Holy wells – natural springs covered by round chambers with domes built in the same manner as the *nuraghi* – add to the variety of prehistoric sites that pepper the island.

> "How prehistoric people engineered this construction is still a mystery"

You might think that seeing one of these prehistoric sites is enough, but they can become positively addictive. Each is a bit different, each reveals a little more – or adds to the puzzle of these ancient peoples. And each is interpreted in a different way, or left as it stands with no interpretation at all, places where 21st-century people can commune undisturbed with the ghosts of their ancient past.

**Nuraghe Losa (opposite); Nuraghe Su Nuraxi (below left); Nuraghe Santu Antíne (right)**

# LIFE'S A **BEACH**

**Sardinia has Italy's most beautiful coastline, and some of the world's most idyllic beaches. Kilometres of blonde sands dip into aquamarine and emerald green waters. Elsewhere, tiny coves and picturesque harbours beg to be explored.**

For many the Costa Smeralda (► 124–125) – Emerald Coast – is the reason that Sardinia is famous. In the 1950s, while yachting in the northeast of the island, the fabulously wealthy Prince Karim Aga Khan IV and his chums became spellbound by the translucent emerald-green waters and romantic little coves. He found a group of businessmen to join him in developing it as a resort that would protect its natural beauty, and so the Costa Smeralda was born. Those jewel-like colours take on every hue from sapphire blue to sparkling turquoise, so dazzling in contrast with the sugar-white sands that you can't help but don your Prada shades. And yet, this is only a tiny area of the island's magnificent wealth of beaches.

### Secret Coves
Great swathes of the Sardinian coast remain uninhabited, with pines, juniper and prickly pears encircling occasional sandy beaches, sea and granite rocks – just as the Costa Smeralda once was. In all directions,

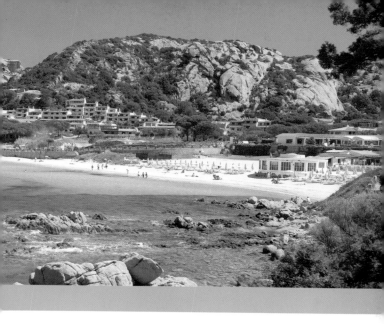

The turquoise waters of Báia Sardinia contrast with its white-sand beach

each area of coast has its own gems. Some are reached only by little paths surrounded by junipers, pine trees, oleander and eucalyptus, others by boat, but most are accessible with an adventurous spirit.

## Superb Beaches
On the west coast, dunes soar and surfers carve their creamy wakes, while at the island's northwestern point white sands shelve from Ísola Asinara into the most brilliant turquoise sea. The pretty northeastern resorts of Palau, Santa Teresa di Gallura, Báia Sardinia and Cannigione might lack the glamour and exclusivity of the Costa Smeralda but many prefer their laid-back feel, and all have beautiful beaches, such as the romantically gorgeous Cala Luna. In eastern part of the Golfo di Orosei (➤ 90–91) is one of Europe's last coastal forests, growing down to a seafront studded with grottoes and spectacular beaches. In the south, emerald-cobalt water laps pinkish-white sand in the Báia Chia, the "Pearl of the South".

## Crowded or Secluded?
All of Sardinia's beaches are open to everyone. While it may be absurd to suggest that anyone could ever tire of the land that gave us Verdi, Vesuvius and Versace, those mainland Italians who want a change of scenery for their summer breaks come to Sardinia in their droves. Yet, even in August at the height of the holiday season, only the main town beaches get crowded. While many UK (and English-speaking) visitors prefer the privacy and space of the quiet coves, Italians like to parade up and down on the more sociable town beaches.

# **Festivals &**
# Carnevale

**The island frequently bursts into life for its festivals. Shrill music fills the air along with the aromas of sweets, bread, herbs, cheeses and wine. If you feel it tugging at your wilder instincts, don't be surprised. Sardinia was born out of rugged traditions and nowhere are these more evident than in its festivals.**

The biggest festivals are usually religious in origin, but others celebrate annual occasions such as the harvest, the turning of the seasons or an historic event. Carnevale (literally "farewell to meat"), usually celebrated in February, sees masked characters, such as the *mamuthones* of Mamoiada (➤ 40, 93) in the Barbágia, enacting battles between devils and animals accompanied by wild dancing, music and, of course, feasting. In picturesque little Bosa (➤ 112), the Carnevale celebrations have lusty, if not blatantly open, sexual connotations.

The island's biggest festival is the religious Sagra di Sant'Efisio in Cágliari. On 1 May the patron saint's image is carried on a cart drawn by decorated oxen from the capital to Nora, where Sant'Efisio was executed. It returns on the night of 4 May accompanied by throngs of people dressed in traditional costume (pictured far left, left and below right) and by the music of the *launeddas*. Unique to Sardinia, this instrument has three pipes made from reed that are played by musicians using their cheeks as a "wind bag". Their sound accompanies many festivals.

**Below: Horsemen in Sássari's Cavalcata Sarda parade**

## Sássari

The second city, Sássari (➤ 104–105), has two major festivals. On the penultimate Sunday in May, the Cavalcata Sarda parade, hundreds of Sardinians in traditional costumes celebrating a victory over the Saracens in AD1000. Afternoon horse races through the streets are followed by evening dancing and merrymaking. During I Candelieri (The Candlesticks) on 14 August, giant wooden candlesticks are paraded through the streets.

## Núoro and San Salvatore

In late August the mountainous interior celebrates with a colourful parade in Núoro (➤ 86–87) for the Festa del Redentore (Christ the Redeemer; ➤ 40, 92). After several days of parades, music, dancing and fireworks, the festival culminates in a procession to the statue of Il Redentore on Monte Ortobene. In September, the Festa di San Salvatore is celebrated by young men running barefoot from Cábras to San Salvatore (➤ 74–75).

## Gastronomic Festivals

There are many food festivals as local delicacies come into season. Among others, the sea urchin festival takes place in Alghero (➤ 106–107) in January, the Sagra dell'Agrume (Citrus Festival) in Muravera and the Sagra delle Castagne (Feast of Chestnuts) fills the streets of Aritzo in October.

# Sardinia's
## Other Islands

**Caught between Africa and Europe, equidistant between the Italian and North African mainlands, Sardinia was well described by the writer D H Lawrence (1885–1930) as being "lost between Europe and Africa and belonging to nowhere". However, Sardinia is not just one island, it is a whole group clustered around the main one.**

Somewhat smaller than Sicily, Sardinia is the second largest island in the Mediterranean, measuring 257km (160 miles) long by 109km (68 miles) wide. Surrounding it are glorious offshore islands, each with its own special characteristics and even history.

In the southwest Ísola di Sant' Antíoco (➤ 56) is Italy's fourth largest island, after Sicily, Sardinia and Elba. Linked by a Roman causeway to the mainland, it was the original site of the Phoenician city Sulci founded in the eighth century BC. While this island's charms are in its abundant prehistoric and early Christian sites, the nearby smaller Ísola di San Pietro (➤ 56) oozes charm of a more recent origin.

Although the Sardinians have no strong tradition as fishermen, the islanders of San Pietro are descended from Genoese coral fishermen brought over in the 18th century. Named after St Peter, who supposedly took shelter during a storm here on his way to Cágliari, the island is

**Sunset at Palau on the Costa Smeralda**

renowned for its excellent fish, especially tuna. A version of Genoese is still spoken in this very picturesque little "piece of Liguria".

## Donkeys and Goats

Other islands take their name from animals, such as Ísola Asinara (Donkey Island; ➤ 110). Lying in the northwest opposite Cape Falcone, the island is uninhabited but has a population of some 250 miniature albino donkeys (pictured below right). Now part of a national park, it's possible visit by guided boat excursions. You may not get to see the little donkeys, but look out for other inhabitants, including falcons, pigs, mouflons and goats.

Ísola Caprera, on the other hand, is named after goats, and is part of the Maddalena Archipelago (➤ 126–127), a cluster of 40 islets and seven main islands off the north coast. Caprera is home not only to goats but also to kestrels, green pines and wild orchids, and to Giuseppe Garibaldi, the national hero of Italian unification in the 19th century, whose former home here is a museum. From La Maddalena, the main island, there are boat trips to inlets and jaw-droppingly beautiful beaches in the archipelago.

## King of the Island

There is even an island with its own king. Beyond Ólbia and the Costa Smeralda the knife edge of the island of Tavolara (➤ 123) rises 564m (1,850 feet) sharply from the sea. Pinky-peach granite rocks, villas and a couple of bars and restaurants are all part of the "Kingdom of Tavolara". Its main inhabitants are peregrine falcons and seabirds. But its king still holds court in his restaurant, Da Tonino, and upholds the title conferred upon his ancestors by Carlo Alberto in 1848.

# The **Wild** West

**Sardinians are among Italy's finest riders, especially in the "Wild West" of Oristano province. They often ride pure-blooded Arab steeds and show off their skills at breakneck speed in spectacular festivals. You can enjoy horse riding and trekking at one of the many equestrian centres.**

## Sa Sartiglia

One of Sardinia's liveliest equestrian festivals is held in Oristano (➤ 68–69) at Carnival time. The town erupts into a frenzy of colourful costumes and thundering hooves over the two-day event. Its origins go back to tournaments, when knights on their galloping steeds had to put their lances through a ring suspended from a rope. Standing upright in their saddles, masked, costumed riders gallop towards a six-pointed star hanging from a rope and try to pierce it with their swords. This is followed by a free-for-all, with daredevil feats of skill.

**Masked riders perform daring feats on horseback during Sa Sartiglia in Oristano**

## S'Ardia

Between 6 and 7 July every year, 100 of the most daring and brave horsemen in the village of Sedilo take part in the wild and frantic S'Ardia (▶ 40). Wielding huge sticks, a group of eight horsemen try to stop the other 92 horsemen from passing their standard-bearer. Shouting crowds line the route and hundreds of riflemen shoot blank cartridges loaded with black dust. Still at full gallop the horsemen circle the church six times while the riflemen continue shooting. The race ends in the steep descent towards the narrow Victory Arch of Constantine. Horses bolt and the excitement of the crowd reaches a crescendo of deafening cheers but no one seems to worry. It is all part of the ritual that makes mainland Italy's *palio* races look like child's play. Sedilo is off the SS131 Abbasanta–Núoro road, a few kilometres from Abbasanta.

## Horse-Riding Excursions

For forays of your own, Oristano is well equipped with riding excursions and courses. Ala Birdi, near Arboréa, has excellent riding facilities for all levels and ages (tel: 0783 80500; www.horsecountry.it).

Elsewhere on the island *agriturismo* farms and larger resorts offer riding to guests and to the public. In Aggius, in the mountains above the Costa Smeralda, Il Muto di Gallura (tel: 079 620 559; www. mutodigallura.com) maintains a stable of Arabian horses that guests can ride, and in the wild landscapes of Ísola Caprera, part of the nearby Arcipélago de la Maddalena, Cavallo Marsalla Centro Ippico (tel: 347 235 9064; www.lamaddalena.it/barabo.htm), has year-round guided horse-trekking trips.

Maneggio Li Nibari (tel: 348 335 0098; www.maneggiolinibari.it), north of Sassari in Stintino, offers horse-riding trips on Cape Falcone from June through October. Also near Sassari, Sardinian Horse Vacations in Valledoria (tel; 328 747 1544; www.sardinianhorse.it) organizes guided trips for six to 10 riders on their Anglo-Arab-Sardinian thoroughbreds, exploring wild landscapes, prehistoric sites and beaches.

**Top: Masked participants in Oristano's Sa Sartiglia**
**Right: The exciting S'Ardia race through the village of Sedilo**

# SARDINIA'S
## Colourful Past

**Even if you know nothing else of Sardinia's past, you may have heard of the mysterious Nuraghic towers that have puzzled archaeologists and travellers for centuries. But that's only one layer of Sardinia's tumultuous history, and there are nearly 5,000 years of it waiting for you to discover.**

That past extends back even farther if you browse through Sardinia's splendid museums, where you'll find stone objects created 10,000 years ago.

From this prehistoric period also come the many *domus de janus*, or "fairy houses" (➤ 9) – tombs cut into rock – and the megalithic burial chambers called "giants' tombs" (➤ 9). You'll find these burial sites around Arzachena (➤ 129–130, Costa Smeralda), at Sant'Andrea Priu (➤ 112) in the Valle dei Nuraghi (south of Sássari), at Necropoli di Anghelu Ruju (north of Alghero) and other sites across the island.

But you're more likely to head first for one of Sardinia's real blockbuster sights – the great stone Nuraghic towers (➤ 8–9) built between 1800BC and 500BC. The most complete and best interpreted of these are Nuraghe Su Nuraxi (➤ 50–51), Nuraghe Losa (➤ 72–73) and Nuraghe Santu Antíne (➤ 112).

Geography doesn't make it practical to visit sights from each era in chronological order, but with a little basic knowledge of the progression of invaders, it's easy to put each in its place as you travel.

**Above: The ancient burial site of Tomba dei Giganti (Giants' Tomb), Li Lolghi**
**Opposite: The Romanesque Basilica della SS Trinità di Saccargia, Sássari**

## Early Visitors

Sardinia's first "invaders" came peacefully and seemed to be welcomed by the Nuraghic people. The Phoenicians arrived as traders and they established towns near the sea, around safe harbours at Nora (➤ 52), Thárros (➤ 70), Sulki and elsewhere. Those sites give you a feel for their cities and their intriguing *tophets* – burial places for children – marked by carved stones. See an outstanding collection of these on site at Sant' Antíoco, where there are also fascinating earlier necropoli caves.

## Pugnacious Punics

The peaceful cultural and material exchange between the Sardinians and Pheonicians ended abruptly with the Punic invasion from Carthage late in the ninth century BC. Islanders joined forces with the Phoenicians, but were no match for the military-minded Carthaginians. Here began the Sardinians' turn inwards as they fled the coast for the security of the mountains. This was also the beginning of the realization that *"furat chi beit dae su mare"* ("he who comes from the sea comes to rob"), which led to a greater emphasis on inland settlements.

But the Carthaginians couldn't sustain control in the face of a highly organized Roman empire on the move, and Sardinia became a colony of Rome in 238BC. Locals retreated further into the wild Barbagia mountains to escape capture.

## GARIBALDI SLEPT HERE

Sardinia's role in Italy's Risorgimento – the mid-19th-century campaign that united various smaller kingdoms into one Italy – is mostly connected to its dynamic leader, Giuseppe Garibaldi (pictured right), considered the father of his country. He chose the island of Caprera for his home, and today Italians visit his modest villa as a national shrine.

### Roman Remains

The Romans made good use of the Phoenician cities at Thárros and Nora, expanding them and building their own on top of them. They built the first roads, connecting Cágliari and Sássari with what would become the route of the modern Carlo Felice highway. They built baths, which you can tour at the hot springs now known as Fordongiánus (➤ 76), and villas. They enlarged the mines that had drawn the Phoenicians here, and brought Christian prisoners to work them, unwittingly introducing Christianity.

In the fourth and fifth centuries, the first Christians were martyred in Sardinia; some of their tombs can be seen in Sássari and Cágliari. Sardinia's only catacombs remain on Ísola di Sant' Antíoco (➤ 56).

"The realization was that 'he who comes from the sea comes to rob'"

When the centre of the Roman empire moved to Constantinople, Sardinia began its own Byzantine period, which lasted from the fifth to the tenth century, during which the Christian presence expanded and the first bishops were appointed. Little remains of this period, save a church in Cábras and San Saturnino in Cágliari. Government was delegated to four judges, the Giudicale.

### Medieval Sardinia

At the beginning of the 11th century, Pisan and Genoan troops were sent to reclaim the island from Arabs, whose increasing raids had again forced locals into the interior. Throughout the early Middle Ages, Romanesque architecture flourished, as Christianity took hold and churches and monasteries were constructed. They range from modest little churches to the most outstanding example, SS Trinità di Saccargia (➤ 111), influenced by the Pisans, whose craftsmen followed the new governing force to the island.

A path leads up to Torre di Longosardo at Santa Teresa di Gallura

## Then Came the Spanish

Italian domination ended in 1297, when Pope Boniface VIII presented the entire island to Jaime II, King of Aragon, beginning four centuries of Catalonian rule. He gave fiefdoms to 400 Catalan families to settle there, many of them around Alghero (▶ 106–107), where the Spanish influence still shows in both Gothic-inspired architecture and the language. Spanish watchtowers dot the coast of Sardinia, built to stave off pirate attacks.

In the early 1700s the island passed to the Piedmont Savoy dynasty, which sent Italian engineers and architects to strengthen fortifications and modernize its cities. Sardinia gradually became more Italian, as Cágliari's neoclassical Marina neighbourhood shows.

## The 20th Century

World War II took a heavy toll on Sardinia, not only in lives lost in battle, but in the devastating bombing of Cágliari. You'll see reminders of that war along the north coast, where concrete bunkers remain of coastal defences. But a more outstanding site is the town of Carbonia, one of the few of Mussolini's planned cities that survives almost intact.

To see the later 20th century's impact, look no further than the pseudo-Aegean enclaves of the Costa Smeralda (▶ 124–125). Planned and built by the Aga Kahn and his associates in the 1960s to create a millionaire's paradise for their own slice of the *dolce vita*, this coast was the darling of the jet set, and became the model for other purpose-built resort towns.

# Sardinian
# Cuisine

**"Sardinian cooking is of a poor nature. It is the cooking of the farmers and shepherds who, in the story of Italy, have never been rich people. Sardinian cooking may be poor in some ways but is extremely rich in others, for example it has flavour, intelligence, versatility and an exotic nature."**

So writes Raffaele Balzano in *Sardegna a Tavola*, a Sardinian cookery book. He might also have added that Sardinia is organic or free range in virtually everything it produces and that many of the delicious flavours come from the wild herbs that carpet the rich pastureland grazed by sheep, cattle and goats.

Just as significant is the fact that locally grown ingredients are not a trendy new idea here – they are integral to Sardinian food culture, and are almost taken for granted. That's not surprising when you remember that Sardinians have aways looked to their own land for sustenance and have never relied heavily on imports.

You'll notice the absence of foreign and ethnic eating places, too; restaurants have to survive after tourist season, and Sardinians prefer

**Left to right: Oak wine barrels; Villa Las Tronas restaurant; spitted pork in Su Gologone**

Sardinian food. Updated and tweaked maybe, and attractivly presented, but true to the local ingredients and traditions. That's not to say that new chefs have not created quite a buzz with stylish new dishes and innovative interpretations of old favourites. Restaurants such as Cágliari's Dr Ampex (➤ 60) and Alghero's Villa Las Tronas (➤ 115) embrace the Sardinian food culture in new and interesting ways, updating it without losing the real essence. And others such as Tenuta Pilastru (➤ 134) in the mountains above the Costa Smeralda are presenting typical local dishes in stylish and up-market settings. Just don't look for a Thai restaurant on every corner.

## Traditional Cooking

Meat forms the basis of traditional Sardinian cuisine, *la cucina tipica Sarda:* lamb, beef, kid goat and wild boar are spit-roasted or grilled with fragant herbs. A real treat is suckling pig *(porceddu)*, which sometimes you must order a day ahead to allow time to massage the skin of the piglet in herbs, olive oil and sea salt before slow-roasting over an open fire, then serving on a bed of fragrant myrtle leaves. You will see other popular menu offerings that are not to everyone's taste: *sa córdula* (roasted or barbecued sheep's entrails), *sanguinaccio* (black pudding made with pig's blood), or *cordula* (lamb tripe stewed, grilled or fried). Horse and donkey meat are popular here, especially served as carpaccio, as is *bue rosso*, a highly prized local red ox.

## Crisp Bread

Although not found in all restaurants, the traditional (and delicious) Sardinian bread is *pane carasau*, wafer-thin and baked twice. Introduced by the Arabs in the ninth century AD, it was adopted by shepherds for its long-keeping qualities. It is delicious served with salt and warm olive oil, and sprinkled with herbs.

## Pasta Sardinian-style

Like everything else on the menu, pasta takes on its own forms in Sardinia. *Fregola* is like pearls of toasted couscous, served in soup or *con arselle* (with clams). *Malloreddus* are small ridged gnocchi-like pasta, prepared with a light tomato sauce and often sausage bits. *Culurgiones* are similar to ravioli, but filled with potato and cheese seasoned with local herbs. A real delicacy is *spaghetti alla bottarga*, made with mullet roe, which

## LONG LIFE AND HAPPINESS

The traditional Sard greeting *A Kent'Annos* ("May you live to 100") is no mere jest. Sardinia has the world's highest percentage of people past their 100th birthday; around 135 people per million live to celebrate it, while the Western average is nearer 75. Sardinians credit the fresh local food and red wine for their longevity.

are dried and grated over the freshly cooked pasta mixed with olive oil. Bottarga is known as "Sardinian caviar" – delicious and expensive.

## Seafood

Although Sardinians are *pastori, non pescatori* – shepherds, not fishermen – seafood is now widely available. Lobster *(aragosta)* is a great favourite, as well as *calamari* (squid) and *polpi* (octopus). Particular delicacies are *ricci di mare* (sea urchins), found on winter menus especially in Alghero.

## Pecorino Rules

Cheese-making is an art form on Sardinia and the delicious pecorino made from ewe's milk accounts for more than three-quarters of Italy's *pecorino romano*. This cheese comes in three forms: the most famous is cooked *pecorino romano*, served grated on pasta and shaved over salads and carpaccio. The semi-cooked *pecorino sardo* is tangy and hard, while the *fiore sardo* is a fresh cheese, white and crumbly. There are others, such as ricotta

> "Meat forms the basis of traditional Sardinian cuisine"

and goat's cheese. For a sweet cheese experience, try *sebada*, like a doughnut, oozing with ricotta cheese and thick, creamy mountain honey.

## Fine Wines

Sardinian wines are among the world's finest, but so prized and produced in such small quantities that vintages often run out quickly. They are therefore not widely exported, so enjoy them while you can in Sardinia. The best reds come mainly from the local Cannonau grape; for whites look for Vermentino and Vernaccia. Some wines are made by the traditional method of leaving the grapes to ferment for up to four weeks, producing a chemical reaction that is claimed to prevent heart disease.

Cannonau wine is made with the oldest grape stock in the world, dating from 1200BC, so may qualify as the mother of all the European wines. Good dessert wines include Moscato and Malvasia, a delicious golden wine from Bosa (► 112). *Mirto* (pronounced "meer-toe"), is made from the myrtle berry, redolent of lavender and blueberry and extremely potent.

## Firewater

The island's strong drink, distilled from the winemaking leftovers, rather like grappa, is known as *su fil'e ferru* – "rod of iron". Locals say that it's named after the practice of marking its hiding place with a piece of wire, but, at around 40 per cent proof, it could also have something to do with the drink's head-splitting strength.

**Opposite top to bottom:** ***Pane carasau*** **is the local crispy bread; café terraces on Via Roma in Cágliari; local cheeses on a market stall**

# A Natural PARADISE

**Shepherds lean on their crooks under the shade of juniper trees watching their flocks graze the aromatic *macchia* vegetation. Eagles nest in the wave-sculpted granite cliffs and wild boar take cover in the forests of cork and holm oak. By the golden dunes, carpets of vivid magenta mesembryanthemums, nicknamed *buon giorno* flowers, open their daisy-like petals to greet the sun.**

Everywhere you go you'll hear the tinkling bells of sheep and goats, the island's most prolific residents. But there are many unique species on this isolated island, such as the mouflon – long-horned wild sheep that are on the brink of extinction on mainland Italy. Giara di Gesturi is home to the *cavallini* – miniature wild horses – and the island of Asinara (► 110) is famous for its little albino donkeys. If you're very lucky, you might spot a *cervo sard*o (Sardinian deer) roaming in the Gennargentu mountains (► 94, 144–146). The World Wildlife Fund has established a reserve on the south coast to protect indigenous deer and wild boar.

### Birdlife
Home to 200 different bird species – a third of the entire number found in Europe – Sardinia attracts many of them with the rich pickings of succulent shrimps in the lagoons. Some like it so much that they have changed their migratory habits, such as the colonies of pink flamingos that now nest and breed in Cágliari's lagoons. Endemic to Sardinia are rare birds such as the golden eagle, peregrine falcon and Eleonora's falcon.

---

### UNDER THE WATER

The sea teems with marine flora and fauna and rich, red coral around the coast of Alghero (► 106–107) and divers prize the north coast from the Gulf of Arzachena to the Gulf of Asinara for its fish-filled reefs. Dolphins are often sighted off Alghero) and around the Maddalena islands (► 126–127).

Left to right: Flamingos; Sardinian red deer; *macchia mediterranea* at Capo Caccia

It's the last place in Europe where the latter are found, and their numbers are increasing dramatically. On the coast road from Alghero to Bosa you may spot some of Italy's largest colony of the endangered griffon vulture.

## Fragrant Flora

All year, but especially in spring and autumn, the island is ablaze with flowers. Roses and thick carpets of brilliantly coloured *buon giorno* flowers are intertwined with exotic orchids, hibiscus, oleander and swathes of bougainvillea. A thick carpet of *macchia mediterranea* (Mediterranean maquis) covers most of the land in a tangled and fragrant profusion of lavender, rosemary, wild fennel, juniper and myrtle.

## Wild Landscapes

Constant winds have sculpted the northeast's rocky landscape into bizarre and otherworldly shapes, especially on Capo Testa, and at the Valle della Luna (Valley of the Moon, ➤ 130) near Aggius. In Parco Nazionale de Golfo di Orosei (➤ 90–91), which protects the pristine southeastern coast and the island's highest peaks, the 2.5km (4-mile) long Gola Su Gorruppu canyon (➤ 93–94) is Europe's deepest at 426m (1,400 feet). Caves, including the breathtaking Grotta di Nettuno (➤ 108–109), carve into the cliffs that guard the island's shore.

# Island
# ARTISTRY

**Haute-couture fashions created from cork, entire towns offering open-air canvases for artists, a mountain village known worldwide for its exquisitely handcrafted knives – the arts are alive and well in Sardinia.**

The island's dynamic artistic tradition dates back to the extraordinary bronze work by Nuraghic peoples, and in the same way that today's chefs are experimenting with new interpretations of the Sardinian cuisine, today's artists draw their inspiration from the materials, techniques and even designs of their ancestors, but express them in new ways.

There's a lot to stimulate ideas. The stunning bronze and gold work in the Museo Archeológico Nazionale (➤ 47) in Cágliari shows off Sardinia's long legacy of metalwork. Knives are legendary, the most famous and desirable of them forged by blacksmiths in Santu Lussúrgiu (➤ 76), north of Oristano. Handles are carved of local horn or wood.

While the knife-makers hold close to original styles and designs, artists elsewhere use these as a starting point for their own creative spirit. But they still favour the native materials prized here for centuries – coarse wool from Sardinian sheep, wood from the chestnut forests, red coral, cork and local plants for baskets.

Even today there is a strong heritage of localized crafts, with certain towns noted for particular products. This is certainly true of the highly prized wool carpets sought by collectors, who still travel to the little stone town of Ággius (➤ 130) high in the mountains near the Costa Smeralda. Woven by hand, much as they have been for centuries, their unique texture is formed by tight loops that stand above the surface, often in contrast to the background. Motifs and colours range from very traditional to striking contemporary designs. The techniques may be old, but the artistry is strictly from the 21st century.

**Left to right: A Suberis Cork dress by Anna Grindi; detail of a mural in Orgosolo; statue of a Nuraghic chief dating from the seventh century BC; mural detail, Orgosolo**

## SHOPPING FOR SARDINIAN ARTS

Sardinian styles and techniques are constantly evolving, which makes shopping for local arts especially exciting. To see the finest in all traditions, from ancient arts to cutting-edge design, seek out one of the ISOLA galleries, located in Cágliari (➤ 62), Núoro (➤ 98) and Oristano (➤ 80).

In other arts, as in rug-making, there is a strong reliance on Sardinian motifs and materials for inspiration, but only as a starting point. Artists and designers continue to create and innovate. In Témpio Pausánia (➤ 130), a town surrounded by cork oak forests, designer Anna Grindi has developed a cork fibre comparable to silk for its lightness and delicacy. Her high-fashion clothes have been acclaimed since they first appeared in 2000.

Not all Sardinia's arts are tactile. The tradition of painted towns began in the late 1960s when artist Pinuccio Sciola began creating murals in San Sperate, near Cágliari. Other Italian and international artists followed, and today San Sperate's streets are decorated by hundreds of these, representing every artistic style. Better known are the political satire murals in a remote and tough-minded village (➤ 93) high in the Gennargentu mountains, where a teacher got his students to paint out their frustrations. More than 150 of Orgosolo's walls are covered in art.

### Timeless Motifs

Nearly a century ago, writer D H Lawrence described the brightly coloured flower and animal designs woven into wool saddlebags. Those traditional motifs he saw can be traced back many centuries, yet he would recognize those same inspirations today. They may be interpreted in different ways, but in equally brilliant shades, the crimson poppy foremost among them. Animal designs, especially deer and mouflon, that were also used in the traditional masks of the mountain village festivals, are echoed in sleek lines in contemporary metal sculpture.

**Weaving local patterns into a carpet in Muravera**

# Finding Your Feet

# First Two Hours

## Arriving by Air

You have three options if you are flying to Sardinia. Cágliari, the international airport serving the capital of Sardinia, is the gateway to the southern coast.

### Cágliari's Airport

- Cágliari's airport is called **Élmas** (tel: 070 210531; www.sogaer.it).
- The airport is 6km (4 miles) northwest of the city centre.
- **Car rental desks** and parking are just outside the terminal; exit the arrivals hall to the right, following signs for Autonoleggi, to a series of small kiosks across the access road, and look for your car rental company's logo.
- Take the SS391 to join the SS131, signposted **Cágliari centre**. If continuing to the southwest, take the SS391 to join the SS130 signposted to Cágliari and Pula.
- The **ARST airport bus** runs frequently daily every 30 minutes from 6am until 11:30pm. The journey takes about 10 minutes. (The last bus for the airport departs from Piazza Matteotti in central Cágliari at 10:30pm.) Buy tickets before boarding, in the small machine opposite the tourist information desk in the arrivals hall, or at the station in Cágliari.
- At the exits on both the ground floor and first floor there are several **taxi companies**. A taxi into Cágliari costs about €25 (tel: 070 400101).

### Alghero's Airport

- Alghero's airport is called **Fertilia** (tel: 079 935039; www.aeroportodi alghero.it). There is a tourist information office in the arrivals terminal (tel: 079 935124; open daily 8:30–1, 3:30–10, but often closes earlier).
- Alghero's airport is served by many domestic airlines servicing mainland Italy, mainly to and from Milan and Rome. Ryanair also has frequent flights here. It is in the northwest of the island and is 10km (6 miles) north of Alghero.
- **Car rental desks** are inside the arrivals terminal, and rental cars are parked outside in the car park opposite the main exit to the airport.
- For **Alghero centre**, turn right out of the airport and take the SS291 to Fertilia, then follow this coast road into Alghero.
- **FdS buses** coincide their departures with flight arrivals from the Italian mainland, about 10 times a day. Tickets are available from the gift and magazine shop, near the tourist office in the arrivals terminal. For travel further afield there are buses from the airport to the main cities of Sássari, Núoro, Oristano and Cágliari, as well as Stintino, Macomér, Castelsardo and Santa Teresa di Gallura. Note that buses to Stintino and Santa Teresa run only from 1 June to 30 September. The main buses are operated by ARST (tel: 800 865 042) and FdS (tel: 079 950458).
- You will find **taxis** outside the exit gates of the arrivals terminal. Taxis into the centre of Alghero cost about €20. There is a 24-hour switchboard (tel: 079 975396 or 079 989 2028).

### Ólbia Airport

- The spanking new airport at Ólbia, now grandly called Aeroporto Internazionale di Ólbia Costa Smeralda (tel: 0789 563444; www.geasar.com), is served by international and charter flights as well as flights from Milan, Rome and Verona. easyJet operates regular flights here. Lying just inland from the northeast coast, it is the gateway to the Costa Smeralda. The airport is 5km (3 miles) southeast of the centre.

- **Car rental desks** lie within easy walking distance of the main arrivals terminal. Look for the sign "Terminal Autonoleggi".
- Take the SS125 **directly into Ólbia** (roadworks are a constant hazard in this city, so there are usually diversions). If travelling to the **Costa Smeralda** take the SS125 from the airport to join the SS131.
- There are **regular services by buses** No 2 (Mon–Sat) and No 10 every 30 minutes (reduced times on Sun), last departure at 7:30pm, to Olbia's central Piazza Regina Margherita. Tickets are available on board or from the ticket machine in the terminal. In summer bus No 6 departs from the airport to Arzachena, Palau and Santa Teresa di Gallura. Buses also go to Cágliari, Núoro, Sássari and, in summer only, to Cala Gonone.
- The **taxi rank** is in front of the arrivals terminal. An average fare into Ólbia is €20.

## Arriving by Sea

- There are many car and passenger ferry companies **from mainland Italy** to Sardinia. The shortest crossings are from Fiumicino and Civitavécchia (Rome), Genoa and Livorno. Most run only during the summer months and it is wise to book well in advance.
- There are **direct routes** from Naples, Palermo, Piombino, Trapani and from Marseille in France and, sometimes, from Toulon.
- There are many **links from Corsica** to Sardinia, the most regular of which is from Bonifacio to Santa Teresa di Gallura.
- For **more information** on all Mediterrean ferry companies, visit www.traghettiweb.it, www.holidays-in-sardinia.com or www.aferry.co.uk

## Tourist Information Offices

- **Cágliari**: Information point, Piazza Matteotti 9 (tel: 070 669255; www.comune.cagliari.it). This is near the waterfront just to the west of Via Roma, and helpful English-speaking staff are on hand Mon–Fri 8:30–1:30, 2–8, Sat–Sun 8–8 (times vary according to season). There is another tourist office at the eastern end of Cágliari's Via Roma at Piazza Deffenu 9 (tel: 070 604241; Mon–Sat 9–1:30).
- **Alghero**: Piazza Porta Terra 9, at the top end of the Giardini Publicci (tel: 079 979054; www.comune.alghero.ss.it; Apr–Oct Mon–Sat 8–8, Sun 9–1; Nov–Mar Mon–Sat 8–2).
- **Núoro**: Piazza Italia 19 (tel: 0784 30083; www.enteturismo.nuoro.it; open Mon–Sat 9–1, 4–7). There is also a useful independent Punto Informa at Corso Garibaldi 155 (tel: 0784 38777; Mon–Fri 9–1, 3:30–7, sometimes also Sat morning).
- **Ólbia**: Via Catello Piro 1 (tel: 0789 21453 or 0789 557601; www.olbiaturismo.it; mid-Jun to mid-Sep Mon–Sat 8:30–1, 4:30–7:30, Sun 8:30–1; mid-Sep to mid-Jun Mon–Sat 8:30–1).
- **Oristano**: Piazza Eleonora d'Arborea 19 (tel: 0783 36831; summer Mon–Sat 9–1, 4–7, Sun 9–2; winter Mon–Fri 9–1, 4–7, Sat 9–1). Associazione Turistica Pro Loco Oristano, Via Ciutadella di Menorca 8 (tel: 0783 70621; www.comune.oristano.it; Mon–Fri 9–12, 4:30–7:30).
- **Sássari**: Via Sebastiano Satta 13 (tel: 079 200 8072; www.comune.sassari.it; Mon–Thu 9–1:30, 4–6, Fri 9–1:30).

---

### Admission Charges

The cost of admission for museums and places of interest mentioned in the guide is indicated by the following price categories:

**Inexpensive** under €3     **Moderate** €3–€5     **Expensive** over €5

# Getting Around

The ideal way to get the most out of Sardinia is by car, but it is also possible to see most of the island's highlights by bus and a few by train, although trains tend to be slower. Cars can be rented from all three airports (➤ 32) or from international and local companies in most main cities and larger towns. Driving in Cágliari in particular can be rather stressful, while Sássari, the second city, has a warren of medieval alleys in the old town, which are best avoided as they are very narrow indeed. Be aware that many of the seaside resorts are pedestrianized in the evenings in summer.

## Driving

- You need a valid **full driver's licence** and, if not a member of the EU, an international driving permit.
- **Contact your insurance company** before departure to ensure you are covered outside your home country.
- If you bring in a **foreign-registered car** you must also carry the vehicle's registration and insurance documents. It is compulsory to carry all your documents while driving in Sardinia as you will be required to present them if stopped by the police.
- To **rent a car** on the island you must be over 21 and have a full valid driver's licence. It is often cheaper to rent a car when you book your holiday as part of a "fly-drive" package. Cars can also be booked through the central telephone numbers or websites of the major rental companies in your country of origin before leaving.
- If you are travelling independently, several of the **airlines have special offers** with car rental companies, best booked at the same time as purchasing your flight.

### Driving Essentials

- **Drive on the right** and overtake on the left. Give way to traffic from the right unless otherwise indicated.
- Wearing **seatbelts** is compulsory in front and back seats.
- It is Italian law to use your **headlights** at all times (including daytime).
- If a driver **flashes his headlights**, it means he's coming through, not that he's conceding you right of way.
- There are no motorways (nor tolls) on Sardinia, but on the main highways the **speed limit** is 110kph (68mph), on secondary roads it is 90kph (55mph) and in built-up areas 50kph (30mph).
- The **main road**, which is mostly dual carriageway, is the SS131 Carlo Felice highway, which runs the length of the country from Cágliari to Sássari and on to Porto Tórres.
- Other SS *(superstrada)* roads are the SS130 running west from the Carlo Felice to Iglésias, and the new dual carriageway that takes you from Sássari part of the way to Alghero. The SS125 (Orientale Sarda) runs down the eastern side of the island from Palau in the north to Cágliari in the south.
- Many of Sardinia's **secondary roads** are very scenic but also very twisty with plenty of hairpin bends. The *strade bianche* (white roads) are often unpaved and little more than rough tracks, more suitable for off-road vehicles than those with a low axle. Be aware that should you have a puncture or flat tyre, you will have to replace it at your own cost.
- **Petrol** is *benzina*, unleaded petrol is *senza piombo*, diesel is *gasolio*. Fuel stations are spaced at relatively regular intervals along the

SS roads, but most close at lunchtime and after 7:30pm. However, many are self-service and take credit cards and euro notes (which must be in good condition and not dog-eared).

- **Parking** can be a nightmare in the big centres. Usually it is restricted to between blue lines and you pay at meters in cities such as Cágliari. Otherwise a parking attendant will issue you with a ticket, which generally is not expensive. Average rates are €0.50 per hour. Don't ever park in a *zona di rimozione* (removal zone), as your car will almost certainly be towed away. If planning to park your car on the road overnight, check that there won't be a market in the immediate vicinity the next day, as you may otherwise find your car trapped.
- If your **car breaks down**, switch on the hazard warning lights and place the red warning triangle (supplied with all rental cars) about 50m (54 yards) behind your vehicle and call the emergency breakdown number (tel: 116).
- If you are **involved in an accident** put out the red warning triangle and call the police (tel: 112/113) and/or ambulance (tel: 118). Do not admit liability or make potentially incriminating statements. Ask witnesses to remain on the scene, exchange names, addresses and insurance details with any other drivers involved and make a statement to the police.

## Trains

- Trains in Sardinia are rather slow, but they are cheap. **Trenitalia** (tel: 892 021 from a land line or 12 892 021 from a mobile phone; www.trenitalia.com) is partially privatized and runs most of the network. The longest trip is from Ólbia to Cágliari.
- Many tourists like to take the *trenino verde* (little green train), which runs through some of the most beautiful parts of the island. It may be slow, but that is part of its appeal as it allows scenic views otherwise impossible to see from the main road. The train connects Cágliari to Árbatax in the south and Sássari to Palau in the north. Perhaps the most scenic trips are from Macomér to Bosa Marina and between Árbatax and Mándas. The *trenino verde* only runs in summer (tel: 070 343112 or toll free 800 460220; www.treninoverde.com).
- **Validate your ticket** before travelling by punching it in one of the machines on the platform.

## Buses

- Sardinia has a **good network of buses** which link not only villages and towns but also beaches (although these, together with those to archaeological sites, only operate during the summer).
- The **main operator ARST** (Azienda Regionale Sarda Trasporti; tel: 800 865 042; www.arst.sardegna.it) has a good service covering routes from the main cities, Cágliari, Sássari, Oristano, Ólbia and Núoro. A trip from Cágliari to Sássari takes about 3 hours 30 minutes and costs about €15. For bus routes and timetables visit www.orariautobus.it

## Ferries

- There are regular ferries from Palau to the island of Maddalena. There are **two main operating companies**: Saremar (tel: 0789 754156; www.saremar.it) and EneRmaR (tel: 0789 708484; www.enermar.it).
- Saremar also operates regular sailings in the **southwest** from Portovesme to Ísola di San Pietro's Carloforte.
- There are also frequent services between Santa Teresa di Gallura and Bonifacio on **Corsica** operated by Saremar and by Moby Lines (tel: 199 303040; www.moby.it).

# Accommodation

With the great exception of the Costa Smeralda, accommodation in Sardinia is cheaper than on the mainland. As the season is short in the resorts (often June to September) early booking is recommended. Some good B&Bs are now on offer, and rural accommodation in *agriturismi* is widely available. Outside the main towns and cities many hotels are closed during the winter.

## Hotels

- **All hotels are graded** by the state from one star to five stars (five being luxury). The criteria for stars are usually based on the number, rather than the standard, of facilities.
- **"High season"** prices usually run from July to the beginning of September, and during this time there may be minimum stays imposed upwards of three days and/or mandatory half, sometimes full board. All prices should be displayed prominently on the premises.
- The old *pensione* classification that used to refer to **a simple hotel** no longer exists, but you may still see one-star hotels calling themselves *pensione*. Usually these premises have shared bathrooms. Two-star hotels have private bathrooms, and rooms in three-star hotels usually have TV and telephone. Four- and five-star properties have correspondingly more facilities and higher quality, while luxury five-stars offer every comfort – reflected in the price. There are several of these in Sardinia, mainly around the Costa Smeralda and nearby resorts, and on the coast near Cágliari. All accommodation prices are much lower out of high season.

## Other Accommodation

- **B&Bs** have become increasingly popular and can be excellent value. Many are in the towns and cities and most have shared bathrooms. For more information contact Bed & Breakfast Sardegna (tel: 0783 216041; www. bebsardegna.it or Sardegna B&B (tel:0783 411660; www.sardegnabb.it).
- *Agriturismi* are usually countryside farmhouses or cottages, often with various activities on offer, such as horseback riding, trekking, biking and excursions to sights of interest. Usually they are more expensive than B&Bs but **many offer home-cooked dinners** with locally grown produce and are often in idyllic rural locations. Contact Agriturismo di Sardegna (tel: 0783 411660; www.agriturismodisardegna.it or www.holidays-in-sardinia.com). Most tourist offices have details of *agriturismi* and, through serendipity, you will stumble across them in the countryside. Smaller ones require booking ahead to be sure someone is there at your arrival.

## Villas and Apartment Rentals

- Several companies offer self-catering in Sardinia, including:
  **Holidays in Sardinia**: www.holidays-in-sardinia.com
  **Interhome**: www.interhome.com
  **Rent Sardinia**: www.rent-sardinia.com
  **Just Sardinia**: www.justsardinia.co.uk
  **Explore Sardinia**: www.exploresardinia.it

---

### Accommodation Prices

The average cost of a double room per night, including taxes:
€ under €90  €€ €90–€155  €€€ €155–€250  €€€€ over €250

# Food and Drink

Food and drink is usually of a high standard in Sardinia and, in many places, is extremely good value. Whether you choose from *la terra* (land) or *il mare* (sea), there is plenty in the authentic Sardinian cuisine found throughout the island to satisfy even the most discerning gourmet.

## Eating Places

■ Similar to mainland Italy, differences between the **various types of restaurant** are no longer so clearly defined. While a *ristorante* used to be an upmarket and expensive establishment and a trattoria was cheap and simple, the two have become increasingly blurred. Pizzerias, too, will often have other dishes, such as pasta and salads, on offer as well as pizzas alone.

■ An *enoteca* is a wine bar that has a good selection of wines by the glass, accompanied by salamis, cheeses and a choice of snacks or light meals. You will also find the odd *birreria* where you can get a beer (or glass of wine) with snacks and light meals.

■ The *gelateria* – or ice-cream parlour – remains perennially popular, as with all Italian destinations committed to glorious *gelato*.

## Eating Hours

■ Bars usually open around 7 for **breakfast** *(prima colazione)*. A cappuccino and *cornetto* (croissant) is the usual Sard fare, which, incidentally, the locals almost never take sitting down. When in Sardinia, stand at the bar and join in.

■ **Lunch** *(pranzo)* is traditionally the main meal of the day. By 1:30 most people are tucking in and it can be a very leisurely affair. After all, everything stops for the siesta and businesses and shops close for up to four hours every afternoon.

■ **Dinner** *(cena)* usually begins late, around 9 (although earlier in rural areas). However, there are plenty of places that cater for visitors who like to dine earlier.

## Meals

■ **Antipasti**, meaning literally "before the meal", are not traditionally Sardinian. However, you will find featured on many menus both meat *(di terra)* and fish *(di mare)* options – usually served in great profusion.

■ *Il primo* is the **first course**, usually pasta or soup *(suppa)*, which is a speciality of Sardinia. Usually containing bread and meat, the *suppa* can be too substantial to be a mere starter for smaller appetites.

■ *Il secondo*, **the main course**, is meat or fish and seafood accompanied by separately ordered vegetables *(contorni)* or salad *(insalata)*.

■ *Dolci* (puddings) and *formaggi* (cheeses) are both Sardinian favourites. There are some delicious traditional pastries and biscuits and the cheeses are among Italy's finest.

■ Meals can be followed by **coffee** – espresso is the Sard and Italian way (never cappuccino after dinner), infusion tea or something stronger, such as grappa or *mirto*, the local liqueur made from myrtle berries.

## Vegetarians

■ The fertile Sardinian land produces **excellent vegetables** but always check that the soups, risottos and pasta dishes are not prepared with meat stock.

- Chicken *(pollo)* and ham *(prosciutto)*, let alone fish, are often **not considered to be proper meat**, so asking if a dish is vegetarian may result in a misleading answer; instead ask what's in it.

## Sardinian Specialities

- Baking the traditional bread, often known as *pane carasau* (➤ 23) is like a rite of passage in Sardinia. Deliciously light, crispy and thin, it is often referred to as "music bread", for it is supposed to be as flat as a sheet of music, *"carta da musica"*.
- Also unique to the island is **mullet *bottarga*** – delicate, amber-coloured roe known as "Sardinian caviar".
- The lush, herb-scented pastureland is perfect for grazing animals, and produces tangy ***pecorino sardo* cheese** (➤ 25), a particular delicacy.

## Drinks

- **Sardinian wines** (➤ 25) are available almost everywhere and are generally good and inexpensive, especially if you opt for a carafe rather than a bottle. Sardinia is known for its **sweet dessert wines**, including Vernaccia, Moscato and Malvasia, as well as the heady red Cannonau, made from an ancient strain of grape.
- As far as **spirits** go, Sardinia's version of grappa, *fil'e ferru* (➤ 25), is a fiery 40 per cent proof; while aromatic *mirto,* made from myrtle berries, is a more potent 60 per cent.
- **Beer** *(birra)* means lager in Italy. It's usually served in two sizes: *píccola* (small, 33cl) or *grande* (large, 66cl). If you ask for *birra nazionale* you'll get Italian Peroni or Sardinian Ichnussa, cheaper than imported brands.

### Cafés and Bars

- It's always less expensive to **stand at the bar** than sit at a table. You pay at a separate cash desk *(cassa)* for your order and then take your receipt to the bar and repeat your order.
- Choosing to **sit at a table** means that the waiter will quickly take your order. What you shouldn't do is pay at the bar and then sit down with your drink. However, once you have elected to have waiter service you can sit for as long as you like – within reason.

## Paying and Tipping

- At the end of the meal ask for the **bill** *(il conto).*
- Almost everywhere you pay a **cover charge** *(pane e coperto)*, which is usually around €2 per person. **Service will also be added** in many restaurants, in which case you don't need to tip. If service is not included then 10 per cent would be an acceptable tip.
- By law, the restaurateur is obliged to give you an **itemized receipt** *(una ricevuta)*, which can be quite useful if the bill is illegible.

## Dress Code

- Sardinians and Italians in general tend to make more of an effort than foreign visitors at **dressing up to eat out**. While most coastal areas are very relaxed, chic restaurants in cities such as Cágliari and Sássari appreciate a little care taken of appearances.

---

### Restaurant Prices

Expect to pay per person for a meal, excluding drinks, tax and tip:
€ under €26          €€ €26–€55          €€€ over €55

# Shopping

You will find crafts, ceramics, coral jewellery, embroidered goods and tasty Sard morsels across the island. In cities such as Cágliari and Sássari you will also find good shops and a couple of department stores with some very glamorous offerings and great accessories, especially shoes.

## Craftware

There is a very rich tradition of craftware (➤ 28–30) on the island, but before heading off to the souvenir shops try to check out the authentic article (and compare prices) in the ISOLA outlets. The Istituto Sardo Organizzazione Lavoro Artigiano (thankfully ISOLA for short) has outlets in places such as Cágliari, Núoro, Porto Cervo, Oristano, Alghero and, especially, Sássari (➤ 104), which has a big shop in the Giardini Púbblici. Here you will find a good range of handicrafts, each piece of which is authenticated.

## Crafts

- **Ceramics** tend to be crafted in simple patterns and colours and some of the best are made around the Costa Smeralda (➤ 124–125), Alghero (➤ 106–107) and Santa Teresa di Gallura (➤ 128).
- Also in the north, Castelsardo (➤ 110–111) has a long **tradition of basketware** made from willow, rush, palm leaves and asphodel.
- Inland, the area around Témpio Pausánia (➤ 130) specializes in splendid **wool carpets** in geometric designs.
- Oliena (➤ 92) has beautiful **embroidered silk shawls**.
- Bosa (➤ 112) is famous for its **lace** – and for its golden Malvasia wine.
- **Jewellery**, especially with the intricate filigree work, is a good buy across the island and, in Alghero (➤ 106–107) especially, you will find it intertwined with the **high-quality coral** for which the town is so famous.
- **Knives** are also a speciality. A classic example is the shepherd's pocket knife, hand-crafted and a real work of art. The finest and most traditional are produced in Santu Lussúrgiu (➤ 76).

## Food and Drink

For gourmet delights, Cannonau wine (increasingly believed to be the elixir of longevity) or sweet Malvasia dessert wine, olive oil, pecorino cheese, mountain honey, *torrone* nougat and Núorese sweetmeats should all be high on the shopping list.

# Entertainment

The island offers a plethora of entertainment from summer open-air festivals and concerts to opera, cutting-edge theatre and dance and pageants and festivities celebrating a prized local delicacy or saint's day (➤ 12–13).

Nightlife throbs around the resorts and in the university towns such as Sássari and Cágliari – and the glitterati and A-list celebrities can often be spotted in the Costa Smeralda in high summer, when it becomes the base of the paparazzi.

## Information

- The tourist offices in individual towns have comprehensive listings on local events. For major cultural festivals, tourist offices in Cágliari, Alghero and Sássari generally have all the details. Also consult visitor centres for up-to-date details of local nightlife as new clubs and bars come and go quite quickly.

## Festivals

There are **festivals for every season** (➤ 12–13). Some celebrate the harvest, many are religious, others involve shows of equestrian expertise, and most are ancient in origin. But all are spectacular and a wonderful opportunity for dancing, feasting and immersing yourself in the infectious Sardinian love of life. The following are just a taster:

- **Carnevale** (Carnival, Feb/Mar) is celebrated throughout the island but Sa Sartiglia in Oristano (➤ 16) is an extraordinary medieval joust of horsemen in glorious, traditional costumes. In Mamoiada (➤ 93) the *mamuthones* procession sees men wearing sinister wooden masks and heavy sheepskin cloaks parading slowly through town tolling mournful cowbells. However, it's all symbolic of good times and rich harvests.
- **Sa Die de Sa Sardigna** (Sardinian Day, 28 Apr) commemorates the Vesper Insurrection (Vespri Sardi) of 1794 that led to the expulsion of the Piedmontese from Sardinia. The leaders' arrest is re-enacted in costume in the San Remy bastion (➤ 46), Cágliari, and musical shows go on late into the evening.
- **Sant'Efisio** (1–4 May) is one of the island's most colourful festivals; it takes place in Cágliari in honour of Sardinia's patron saint (➤ 62).
- **Cavalcata Sarda,** Sássari (penultimate Sun in May) is a costumed pageant celebrating a victory over the Saracens in AD1000, followed by a spirited horseback gallop through the streets (➤ 13).
- **S'Ardia,** Sedilo (6–8 Jul) is a spectacular but dangerous horse race between Oristano and Núoro, accompanied by gunshots and thousands of spectators (➤ 17).
- **I Candelieri,** Sássari (14 Aug) sees giant timber "candles" paraded through the streets in the city's big feast (➤ 13, 104).
- **Sagra del Redentore** (➤ 13, 92) Monte Ortobene (29 Aug), is celebrated with a torch-lit procession and fabulous traditional costumes.
- **Festa di San Salvatore** (first Sun in Sep), involves the Barefoot Race, 8km (5 miles) to San Salvatore from Cábras and back again (➤ 74).

## Sports

- **Swimming** is good all around the coast.
- **Windsurfing or kite-surfing** are popular everywhere, although the winds are especially good on the north coast. The west coast has some terrific surf at the beaches around Buggerru.
- **Sailing** is the royal pastime – especially on the Costa Smeralda – where it is possible to rent a yacht if you haven't brought one with you.
- **Snorkellers and divers** will find an underwater paradise in the limpid waters, and there are many schools and PADI-registered diving outfits scattered around the island, especially around the Golfo di Orosei (➤ 90–91).
- For **golf enthusiasts** Sardinia has two of Europe's most beautiful 18-hole courses – Pevero Golf Club at the Costa Smeralda's Cala di Volpe and Is Molas Golf Hotel at Santa Margherita di Pula.
- There is wonderful mountain terrain to be explored and **hiked** over, especially in the Gennargentu and Sopramonte mountain ranges.
- **Bolted rock climbing** is very popular around Cala Gonone.
- **Horse trekking** (➤ 17) is very popular in the Barbágia region, and plenty of seaside resorts offer the opportunity to canter along the sands on the sparkling seashore.

# Cágliari and the South

# Getting Your Bearings

Sardinia's capital Cágliari is a busy, salty port – the island's largest city by far – and a tantalizing pot pourri of ancient and modern. This southern part of the island was especially attractive to the Phoenicians, Carthaginians and, of course, Romans, and the area is peppered with souvenirs of their stay. But the Nuraghic civilization was here, too, leaving behind their most complete settlement at Su Nuraxi. And then there are the beaches – some of the island's most beautiful – and all within striking distance of the city.

**Page 41:**
**A narrow street in Cágliari**

Known as "Casteddu" (the castle) in the Sardinian language, Cágliari perches on top of a hill overlooking its beautiful gulf, the Bay of Angels.

Most of the white limestone city walls are intact and the impressive effect of the warm Mediterrean sunlight reflecting on the dazzling city moved British author D H Lawrence to compare the city to a "white Jerusalem" in his book *Sea and Sardinia*. The Castello quarter is the old town and also home to the island's best archaeological museum, the fascinating Museo Archeológico Nazionale. The lower town, or Marina quarter, is the perfect place for strolling and dining in the maze of little streets behind the Via Roma. The city outskirts may be sprawling and industrial but, even there, flamingos preen and birdlife flocks in to the lagoons, not so far from the airport itself.

Inland the huge prehistoric site of Nuraghe Su Nuraxi looms up from the hill country of La Marmilla. To the west is the wildly beautiful Costa Verde, while the Costa del Sud has kilometre upon kilometre of white sand and dunes on the approach to Nora and its evocative ruins.

# In Four Days

**If you're not quite sure where to begin your travels, this itinerary recommends a practical and enjoyable four days exploring Cágliari and the south of the island, taking in some of the best places to see using the Getting Your Bearings map on the previous page. For more information see the main entries.**

# Day 1

**Morning**
Travel to – or wake up in – Cágliari. Visit the tourist office, then walk around ⬛ Il Castello Quarter (➤ 46–47). Enjoy a coffee at the Caffé Arsenale, Piazza Arsenale, just by the entrance to the museum, and then visit the Museo Archeológico Nazionale (➤ 47).

**Lunch**
Have a picnic by Bastione San Remy (➤ 46; left) or try for a table outside in the De Candia bar/restaurant (Via Marco de Candia 1–3, just by the Bastione). Good snacks are available (and at night there's often live music from 11pm).

**Afternoon**
Head for the beach at ⬛ Poetto (➤ 54–55) and admire the boats at Marina Píccola (➤ 54–55) on the western end.

**Late afternoon and evening**
Stroll around Cágliari and indulge in some retail therapy. Via Manno is good for fashion shops, while the department store Rinascente is on Via Roma. Have dinner at Dal Corsaro (Marina quarter, ➤ 60; right) or at Dr Ampex (➤ 60).

# Day 2

**Morning**
Take the SS131 (Carlo Felice Highway) north in the direction of Sanluri and then the SS197 northeast signposted Barúmini. Su Nuraxi is just outside it.

Have a coffee in the bar across the road, then join a guided tour of **4 Su Nuraxi** (➤ 50–51).

**Lunch**
Try Barúmini's Sa Lolla Albergo Ristorante (➤ 61).

**Afternoon**
Drive south on the SS197 towards Sanluri. Continue past San Gavino to Gúspini and take the scenic SS126 past Árbus and on to the Costa Verde. Stop for a drink at Buggerru (off the SP83) and admire the dramatic seascape. Continue down to Sant' Antíoco and, if time, take the ferry across to **13 Ísola di San Pietro** (➤ 56; Carloforte, right).

# Day 3

**Morning**
Take the SS195 running along the **15 Costa del Sud** (➤ 57) to Chia and relax on the beach.

**Lunch**
Try a pizza or pasta alfresco at Le Dune (➤ 61).

**Afternoon**
Visit the archaeological site of **5 Nora** (➤ 52). Stay overnight at Chia.

# Day 4

**Morning**
Take the scenic coastal road to **2 Villasimíus** (➤ 48) or the direct road SS125 east of Cágliari to the Monte dei Sette Fratelli (➤ 49).

**Lunch**
Have a picnic or lunch at Le Vecchie Carceri, Castiádas.

**Afternoon**
Relax in Villasimíus and/or take a boat trip to **10 Ísola dei Cávoli** (➤ 55) and **11 Ísola Serpentara** (➤ 55–56).

**Evening**
Start the evening with an *aperitivo* at the Plaza Café on Piazza Incani in the heart of Villasimíus. Stay overnight in the town.

# ⓪ Cágliari's Castello Quarter

Known as the *città d'acqua e di luce* – city of water and light – the Sardinian capital is a vibrant place. The first inhabitants settled here at the end of the third millennium BC and its monuments trace the island's history from its ancient origins to the present day. The Phoenicians called it Kàralis, meaning "rocky place", and when you look out from the dramatic ramparts over the limestone hills, this name seems very apt.

The historic centre within the bastioned walls is known as the Castello, or "Casteddu", as the locals refer to the whole city. It is compact and, although steep, is relatively easy to walk around. Defences were erected here by the Pisans after they took over the Byzantine city in 1217, though the present walls are Catalan and Piedmontese extensions. West of the Bastione San Remy, next to the university, the white 14th-century Pisan **Torre dell'Elefante** is one of the only two remaining towers. Look for the sculpted elephant at the base, and the portcullis, which was once festooned with the heads of executed prisoners. A climb to the top rewards with altogether more savoury views from the terrace.

**Above:**
**Cattedrale di Santa Maria and city walls, Cágliari**

**Top right:**
**Detail of the facade of the cathedral**

In the centre of Castello is the **Cattedrale di Santa Maria**. It was originally built in the 13th century, but few vestiges of its former Gothic glory remain after rebuilding in the 17th century and a makeover for the 2000 Jubilee. D H Lawrence commented that it had gone through "the mincing machine of the ages, and oozed out baroque and sausagey". However, there are still some treasures inside, including the two stone pulpits (originally one) on each side of the main doors, which were carved for Pisa cathedral in 1162 and presented by the Pisans to Cágliari in 1312.

## Museo Archeológico Nazionale

Here you'll find the island's most important collection of artefacts from **prehistoric to Roman times**. Spanning three floors, the museum's first level is devoted to the pre-Nuraghic millennia, including obsidian tools and little round fertility stone goddesses – part of the Great Mother Goddess cult often found in "fairy houses" (➤ 9) – bronze statuettes used as votive offerings, and jewellery, from necklaces of fox teeth (*canini di volpe*) to an exquisite filigree gold necklace and earrings dating from the fourth century BC.

## Largo Carlo Felice

This is Cágliari's most **important street**, where, in late spring and autumn, jacaranda trees put on a breathtaking display. At the southern end is Via Roma, lined with cafés, bars and elegant shops, and the place to watch the evening *passeggiata*.

### TAKING A BREAK

Have a drink or snack at the **Caffè degli Spiriti** on the terrace at Bastione San Remy and admire the lovely views.

✚ 170 B4

**Torre dell'Elefante**
✉ Via Università 🕐 May–Oct Tue–Sun 9–1, 3:30–7:30; Nov–Apr 9–4:30
🖐 Moderate

**Cattedrale di Santa Maria**
✉ Piazza Palazzo ☎ 070 663837 🕐 Mon–Sat 8–12:30, 4–7, Sun 8–1, 4–8

**Museo Archeológico Nazionale**
✉ Piazza dell' Arsenale ☎ 070 655911 🕐 Tue–Sun 9–8 🖐 Moderate
🚌 Circolare

---

### CÁGLIARI'S CASTELLO QUARTER: INSIDE INFO

**Top tip** Of the two towers, the **Torre dell'Elefante** is the better choice to climb, rather than the Torre San Pancrazio, as it has **access to the top terrace**.

# 2 Villasimíus

Lying in the far southeastern corner of the island, framed by *macchia* and pines, the former fishing village of Villasimíus is now a popular resort almost unfairly endowed with beautiful beaches nearby.

The main street in Villasimíus, Via Umberto I, widens out at the two main squares, Piazza Gramsci and Piazza Incani, at the heart of town. The **tourist information centre** is located at Piazza Gramsci – a good place to pick up information on boat trips to the islands of Cávoli and Serpentara.

Off Via Umberto I on Via Frau, the **Museo Archeológico** showcases local finds from Phoenician and Roman settlements and a wreckage recovered from a 16th-century sunken ship.

Spiaggia Simius is the nearest beach, 1.5km (1 mile) down Via del Mare, its fine, white sand lapped by azure-green shallow seas. From here there are magnificent views of the offshore islands of **Cávoli and Serpentara**. Towards the south, the beach joins the Spiaggia Porto Giunco-Notteri, separating the sea from the lagoon of Notteri, which is frequently home to pink flamingos. On the western side the sands of Spiaggia del Riso are reminiscent of grains of white rice, hence the name "Riso" (rice). In fact they're minuscule pieces of translucent quartz.

The headland of **Capo Carbonara**, complete with old fortress and harbour, is the most southeasterly point of Sardinia. The high coast road north to Costa Rei is extraordinarily scenic, with glorious beaches along it.

### TAKING A BREAK

The **Café del Porto** (➤ 60) by the marina is a good bet.

✚ 169 D1

**Museo Archeológico**
✉ Via Frau ☎ 070 7930290 ◷ Mid-Jun to mid-Sep Tue–Fri 10–1, 9–12; mid-Sep to mid-Jun Tue–Thu 10–1, Fri–Sun 10–1, 5–7

**View along the shore to the old fortress**

# 3 Sárrabus

Only a few miles east of the capital, the Sette Fratelli mountains rise abruptly into a wild region of dense forests and *macchia*, a sharp contrast to the urbane pleasures of Cágliari and the sybaritic beach life of Villasimíus.

The rugged peaks of the **Monte dei Sette Fratelli** (Seven Brothers) rise to 1,023m (3,356 feet). They are inhabited by some of the island's last remaining deer, who take cover under the mantle of fragrant *macchia*, cork and holm oak. The area is also rich in wild boar, hare and birdlife.

The winding and very scenic SS125 east of Cágliari goes north to the Monte dei Sette Fratelli. About 29km (18 miles) out of Cágliari you come to a left fork for **Burcei**, famous for its cherry blossom in May. Opposite this turn-off is the Caserma Forestale. Here you can obtain maps of all the walks in the area, ranging from short mile-long loops to all-day treks.

To the northwest of Villasimíus, off the SP17 at **Castiádas**, there is a very good access point for the Monte dei Sette Fratelli, and the Cooperativa Monte dei Sette Fratelli here has a huge array of excursions on offer.

**The peaks of the Monte dei Sette Fratelli**

The town was a penal colony in the 19th century, and the buildings have now been restored.

The Sárrabus meets the sea at the little-known **Costa Rei**, a long string of glorious golden sand beaches with far less development than those closer to Cágliari. These are reached by driving north along the coast from Villasimíus to Muravera.

### TAKING A BREAK

Seek the shade of parasols on the terrace of **Marina Gio** (► 61) enjoying a bounteous lunch overlooking the beach at Marina di San Giovani, just south of Muravera.

# ❹ Nuraghe Su Nuraxi

In Sardinian dialect, *su nuraxi* means simply "the *nuraghi*". This site is the largest and most important Nuraghic complex on the island and is a UNESCO World Heritage Site. It looks like a beehive, surrounded by a honeycomb of the remains of buildings.

The complex at Barúmini, which was extended and reinforced in the first half of the first millennium BC under the Carthaginians, is the **finest and most complete example** of this remarkable form of prehistoric architecture. Visible for miles around, the main central tower of Su Nuraxi rises over a small plain, surrounded by other *nuraghi* to form a star-shaped system. Yet for centuries it was buried among the other hills of the Marmilla area. It wasn't until 1949 that excavation began, by the Sardinian archaeologist Giovanni Liulli, who became convinced that the hummock concealed Nuraghic treasures. It took six years to uncover it and excavations still continue today.

Looking down inside the main tower

## Guided Tours

Tours depart from the ticket office and bookshop on the half hour in the company of a guide who is usually multilingual. You are not allowed to walk on the site unaccompanied as it is potentially quite dangerous. The terrain is very uneven and some scrambling up and down in confined spaces is necessary.

The oldest section is the huge **three-storey central tower** that was originally some 18m (60 feet) high but now rises to 13.7m (45 feet). It is estimated to date back to 1500BC and is thought to have been buried by the Sards during the time of the Roman conquest. What remains today is remarkably well preserved.

## NURAGHE SU NURAXI: INSIDE INFO

**Top tips** You need to have strong shoes for negotiating the **rough terrain** of Su Nuraxi, and the site is not at all suitable for those who find walking difficult.
- In Barúmini the Casa Zapata (tel: 070 936 8476) has some finds on display from Su Nuraxi, but the most comprehensive display is at the **Museo Archeológico Nazionale in Cágliari.**

**Hidden gem** Nearby (1km/0.6 mile west of Barúmini) is Sardegna in Miniatura (below), a **miniature model island** of Sardinia complete with scaled-down versions of huts in a Nuraghic village and a play area, which is ideal for children (open Easter–Sep daily 9–5; Oct–Easter Sun and holidays only).

**Sardengna in Miniatura near Barúmini**

Built of dark basalt blocks, the central tower is believed to have been **constructed from volcanic stone** transported from 10km (6 miles) away. The scale of Nuraghic constructions varied greatly, depending on the function and importance of the buildings. Here, the fortress had a bastion with four towers at the corners.

The bastion towers led to the courtyard through long corridors. The lower chamber at the end of a corridor is of the "tholos" type, where a "false cupola" was built by laying successive stones so that each course overhangs the previous one. To get here you have to negotiate narrow, dimly lit passageways and steps hewn from the rock.

From the top there are **superb views** of the whole site and of the more than 200 horseshoe-shaped roofless buildings of the surrounding Nuraghic village, some of which have now been reconstructed.

### TAKING A BREAK

Have a coffee or a snack in the **bar** opposite the entrance to Su Nuraxi.

➕ 168 A5  ✉ Su Nuraxi, Barúmini  ☎ 070 936 8128  🕐 Daily 9–dusk. Entry by guided tour only, running on the half hour  💷 Expensive

# 5 Nora

**In a setting surrounded by water, Nora is a time capsule of the island's early invaders. Phoenicians, Carthaginians and Romans all traded and lived here, and remains of two of those cultures are visible today.**

Nora was the first city on the island to be founded by the Phoenicians in the eighth century BC. Strategically positioned on the Capo di Pula promontory, it had three harbours, so ensuring that at least one of them would be sheltered from the winds. It was expanded by the Romans to become the most important city in Sardinia, but began to decline in the fifth century AD as increasing Arab raids forced inhabitants to the more easily defended hills of Cágliari. It was previously thought that the town was abandoned because of rising sea levels, but although a small part of the city now lies underwater, recent studies have proven that to be an unlikely reason for abandoning the site.

It is an evocative place, encircled by fragrant umbrella pines and overlooking a pretty beach. Most of the **remains date to the Roman period**.

Highlights include the **theatre**, the only one on the island that staged plays rather than gladiatorial shows (it is still used for open-air concerts in summer), and the **Thermae** (baths) of which there were four.

**Ruins of the Roman amphitheatre**

Traces of Nora's Phoenician past are still visible. The earliest evidence found here are the steps from a **Nuraghic well**, near the sea baths.

A long beach connects the historic site to the Byzantine-style church of Sant'Efisio, built in 1089 on the site where the saint was beheaded by Romans in AD303. The church is the destination of processions from Cagliari on 1 May (➤ 40, 62).

**TAKING A BREAK**

There's a restaurant and bar nearby, at **Sant'Efisio church**.

---

✚ 167 E1 ⊠ Zona Archeológica ⏰ Daily 9–7:30 💰 Moderate. Entrance also gives admission to the Museo Archeológico in Pula

# At Your Leisure

## 6 Orto Botánico

Under a shady ficus tree, opposite a lily pond and fountain, the bronze bust of the founder, Patrizio Gennari (1820–97), greets you. This is one of Italy's most famous botanical gardens and has more than 500 species of tropical and Mediterranean plants. Among the exotic plants and trees bearing lemons the size of melons are the remains of Roman wells and cisterns and an interesting display of medicinal or "curative" plants. It is a cool Cágliari retreat for a stroll among some prized specimens.

🔒 170 A5 ✉ Viale Sant' Ignazio da Láconi
🕓 Mon–Sat 8–1:30, 3–6, Sun 8–1:30
💶 Inexpensive. Guided visits in English sometimes available

## 7 Villanova

Villanova, on the eastern side of Cágliari, is modern and bustling and has a vibrant artisan quarter. At its heart, the Via S Giovanni is door-to-door carpenters, inlayers, restorers, leather workers, even barbers, all plying their trade. This area is also home to some of Cágliari's most famous churches.

The church of San Domenico was built in 1254. Severely bombed in 1943, it was largely rebuilt in 1954. However, there are still interesting parts of the old structure (dating from 1400 to 1580). These remains include the Chapel of the Rosario (1580) and the elaborate Chiostro (cloister), three sides of which are fortunately intact, including the crypt, which contains parts of the late-Gothic building.

The Basilica di San Saturno on Piazza San Cosimo is one of Sardinia's oldest churches. An example of Palaeo-Christian architecture, it was built in the fifth century in dedication to the Christian martyr Saturninus, who was killed on this spot during Emperor Diocletian's reign in AD304. It was later converted as a basilica in 1089. Recent excavation has revealed

Window balconies in Villanova

that it was originally a pre-Christian and then a Christian necropolis. The interior is stark and devoid of any decoration, but you can see the necropolis through the glass walls on either side of the nave.

🔒 170 C5

### San Domenico

✉ Piazza San Domenico ☎ 070 662837
🕓 Admission by appointment only 💶 Free

### San Saturno

✉ Piazza San Cosimo (on the corner of Via Dante) ☎ 070 659869 🕓 Tue–Fri 9–1
💶 Free

## 8 Castello di San Michele

The Spanish fortress stands atop a hill on the northwestern outskirts of Cágliari. It started as a Byzantine tower in the 10th century and was expanded to include a Romanesque church (11th century), Pisan walls (13th century) and, under the Catalans, two more towers (14th century). Its chequered

**Castello di San Michele is on the outskirts of Cágliari**

### ❾ Poetto and Marina Píccola

For sun, sand and relaxation, Poetto beach is the magnet for the local Cagliaritani and visitors alike. The 6km (4-mile) stretch of soft, white sand lapped by clear, turquoise sea is beautifully framed by the mountains of the Sárrabus and Capo Carbonara. It is also backed by the lagoon of Molentargius, frequented by flamingos and many other species of wetland bird.

At the southern end a rocky promontory, known as the Sella del Diávolo (Devil's Saddle), rears above the marina. Legend has it that the Archangel Gabriel won a tussle with the Devil here and threw him off his *sella*, chasing him away with his band of angels – also giving the name Golfo degli Ángeli (Angels' Bay) to the Gulf of Cágliari. Loungers and parasols are available for rent (€10 each) and there are plenty of water sports available such as windsurfing, pedalos and canoes. The beach bristles with bars and cafés.

The Quartu Sant'Elena beach is the continuation of Poetto towards the east. At the other end, the westernmost point of Poetto, Marina Píccola is also the liveliest part of the beach. Protected by the Sella del

history has included a spell as a luxurious residence belonging to the 15th-century Carroz family, who "acquired" decorative stone and marble pieces from the Basilica di San Saturnino to repair the castle's walls. During the great plague of 1652 it was a victims' hospital, and later a general hospital from 1820 to 1848. It was taken over by the Fascists in the 1930s and is now an exhibition centre. The views from the castle are spectacular – right across the Bay of Cágliari and the Campidano Plain – and best enjoyed at sunset.

➕ 168 B2 ✉ Via Sirai ☎ 070 500656 🕐 Jun–Sep Mon–Sat 10–1, 5–10, Sun 10–1, 3–6; Oct–May daily 10–1, 3–6 🚌 City bus 5 💷 Moderate

**Brightly painted beach huts at Poetto**

**A view across to the lighthouse on the Ísola dei Cávoli**

Diávolo promontory, the picturesque yacht basin is a fashionable local meeting place and sailing centre. In high summer there's a concert area and an open-air cinema.

🚌 168 B2 🚍 Buses PF, PQ from Piazza Matteotti

## 🔟 Ísola dei Cávoli

South of Villasimíus, the Capo Carbonara Protected Marine Area is a sea reserve protecting the coastline from Capo Boi to Punta de is Cappuccinus, including the idyllic little islands of Cávoli and Serpentara. However, it's still possible to take a boat trip to these islands as part of an excursion. The Ísola dei Cávoli is rather unpoetically named "cabbage island", belying its castaway feel. A type of wild *cávoli* (cabbage) plant grows here in profusion together with Mediterranean *macchia*, wild carrot, garlic, myrtle and sea fennel. From the granite rocks there are magnificent views across to swathes of white beaches as far as the Gulf of Cágliari. The rough, jagged coastline of granite rock is interspersed with tiny beaches, and the sea teems with marine life as it is now a protected marine park. Submerged in the water off the coast of the Ísola dei Cávoli lies a statue of the Madonna of shipwrecked sailors, to whom a feast day is dedicated, the Festa della Madonna del Naufrago. Every year on the second Sunday of July a procession of boats reaches the location and a scuba priest recites a prayer at a depth of 10m (33 feet).

🚌 169 D1 🚤 Boat trips on the sailing schooner *Matilda* 340 067 6054/330 638234 🕐 From the marina/port daily in season (weather permitting) 10:30–4:30, with two stops for swimming 💶 Expensive, lunch and drinks included

## 🔟 Ísola Serpentara

The island takes its name from its elongated shape as it snakes out along the sea, or possibly from the rare fly-trapping plant that flourishes on the island, the snake flower or *Helicodiceros muscivorus*. Like Cávoli, the island is granite rock covered with *macchia* and there is also a Spanish tower. It is another perfect perch for the seagulls.

Cávoli island has been classified a Zone B protected area, which means scuba diving, fishing and unauthorized navigation are normally forbidden. Swimming and navigation with small, low-speed craft are permitted but fishing and scuba diving need official permission. The area of sea between Serpentara and Sardinia has been declared a Zone A Marine Park, which means it is totally protected and navigation is not even allowed.

🚩 169 E1 🚢 Boat tours around Serpentara and the beaches aboard *Fiore de Maggio* depart Porto Turistico di Villasimíus, Wharf D ☎ 340 486 2894 🕐 May–Sep daily by advance booking 💶 Expensive

## 🔢 Costa Verde

The southwestern Costa Verde (Green Coast) covers the areas of Gonnesa, Iglésias, Buggerru and Árbus. It is characterized by vast sand dunes – among the largest in Europe – sculpted along the shores by the frequent northwesterly winds.

There is not a great deal to see in Árbus except the Museo del Coltello Sardo, which is devoted to the Sardinian knife, with its distinctive round, flat blade. Outside is the largest knife in the world, 3.35m (11 feet) long and named in the *Guinness Book of Records* since 1986.

Just north of Buggerru is one of the island's not-to-be-missed golden beaches – **Spiaggia San Nicolò**, which is never crowded.

🚩 166 C5

### Museo del Coltello Sardo
✉ Via Roma 15, Árbus ☎ 070 975 9220; www.museodelcoltello.it 🕐 Mon–Fri 8–12, 4–8 💶 Free

## 🔢 Ísola di San Pietro

The very pretty Ísola di San Pietro is reached by a half-hour ferry ride from the island of Sant' Antíoco. As the first sight of Carloforte, San Pietro's only town, comes into view, you could easily imagine yourself to be in mainland Italy's Liguria. Pastel-coloured houses cluster around the harbour and little alleys, and the main street bears the name Via Genova. None of this is surprising when you discover that a colony of Genoese coral fishermen came here to settle in 1738; a version of old Genoese is still spoken today.

San Pietro is the perfect place for relaxing and taking a boat trip around the dramatic coastline and **Punta delle Colonne** rock formations.

🚩 166 A3 🚢 Ferries from Sant' Antíoco depart from Calasetta, every hour with Saremar ferries; less frequently with Delcomar 💶 Foot passenger inexpensive, car moderate

## 🔢 Ísola di Sant' Antíoco

The island is a microcosm of nearly everyone who has controlled Sardinia, with neolithic, Byzantine, Phoenician and Roman sites and artefacts to prove it. Locate the prehistoric sites on the interactive map at the excellent Antiquarium museum, whose collections include all the finds from the adjoining *tophet* where eighth-century BC Phoenicians and later Carthaginians buried the cremated remains of children.

From the little ethnographic museum, guides will take you to explore the astonishing Punic-era tombs carved into bedrock underneath the Savoy castle, some recycled as homes. More Phoenician-Punic connected tombs later became

**The estuary at River Piscinas on the Costa Verde**

Torre di Chia stands above Báia Chia, one of the best beaches in Europe

catacombs, and can be seen under the Basilica di Sant' Antíoco Martire below the castle.
🔲 166 B2

## Parco Archeológico
✉ Via S. Moscati, Sant' Antíoco ☎ 0781 800596; www.archeotur.it 🎫 Museum and *tophet:* daily 9–7 (may close for lunch in winter). Villaggio Ipogeo and fortress: Apr–Sep daily 9–8; 1–15 Oct 9–1, 3:30–8; 16 Oct–Mar 9:30–1, 3–6

## 🅖 Costa del Sud
Southwest of Cágliari, the coastal road along the Costa del Sud is one of the island's most scenic. Punctuated by rugged cliffs, coves and Spanish watchtowers, the snaking coastline is awash with sparkling blue seas and soft, sugar-white sands and dunes.

Rated among the top five in Europe, the beaches at Báia Chia are beautiful, with soft white sand and dunes, partly flanked by lagoons rich in local flora and fauna and backed by juniper trees. Walk up to the Torre di Chia – a 16th-century stone tower that was once part of an imposing network of sea defences to repel Turkish pirates and invaders. The Spiaggia Sa Colonia is one of the most glorious beaches and overlooks the site of the ancient Phoenician-Punic city of Bithia.

Between Chia and Pula, the Spiaggia di Santa Margherita has

Forte Su Pisu on the island of Sant' Antíoco was built in 1812

a long white stretch of sand and a backdrop of scented *macchia* and pines. Capo Cala Cipolla is next to Báia Chia and only accessible by foot, but its picturesque beach and cliffs make it worth the effort. It also has seven reefs – a paradise for scuba divers. This 20km (12-mile) stretch of coast is accessed by heading west from Cágliari along the SS195 onto the Strada della Costa, which follows the unfurling coastal panoramas.
🔲 167 D1 ✉ Porto Turistico di Cala Verde, Santa Margherita di Pula ☎ 070 924 1042 (tourist office)

### Diving
✉ Roberto Spinelli & Stefano Barbareschi, c/o Grand Hotel Chia Laguna, Località Chia, Domus de Maria

# Where to...
## Stay

**Prices**
Expect to pay per double room, per night:

€ under €90    €€ €90–€155    €€€ €155–€250    €€€€ over €250

## CÁGLIARI

### Hotel AeR Bundes Jack Vittoria €

In the heart of town, on the Via Roma with sea views, this historic building houses a characterful two-star hotel on the third floor (with a lift). Established in 1938, the high ceilings, Murano glass, antique tiles, balconies, air-conditioned and spotless rooms and bathrooms give this family-run establishment more than a feel of faded elegance. For the best views, choose the sea-facing rooms with balconies, which carry a supplement. The family also runs the Bed and Breakfast Vittoria next door.

➕ **170 B4** ✉ Via Roma 75
☎ 070 657970; www.hotelbjvittoria.it

### Hotel Calamosca €€

This large beach hotel has an excellent position right on the seafront. It overlooks a cove near the lighthouse on Capo Sant'Elia and is very convenient for Poetto. Most rooms have a balcony overlooking the garden or bay; the sea-facing rooms have a small supplement but are the ones to choose. There is a pleasant garden and direct access to two beaches, one of which is the hotel's private rocky beach at the bottom of the garden, the other is public with a beach bar. The hotel is about 2km (1 mile) from the centre of the town and the port, and 10km (6 miles) from the airport of Élmas.

➕ **167 F3** ✉ Viale Calamosca
☎ 070 371628; www.hotelcalamosca.it

### T Hotel €€€

This is Cágliari's first designer hotel. The 15-floor steel and glass round tower opened in October 2005 after the famous Milanese architect Marco Piva had woven his magic, inspired by the colours of the south. There are 207 very stylish rooms themed on four different colours – vibrant orange, fiery red, relaxing green and tranquil blue – and all have spacious, airy bathrooms, glistening mosaic tiles and huge mirrors. The T Bistrot, combining style with minimalist decor and good food, has become a popular meeting point, especially for Sunday brunch. There are also the T Restaurant and T Bar. The beauty and wellness centre is complete with an indoor pool. The hotel is on Piazza Giovanni XXIII in the heart of Cágliari, near the Teatro Lirico, and has underground parking.

➕ **167 F3** ✉ Via dei Giudicati 66
☎ 070 47400; www.thotel.it

## VILLASIMÍUS

### Pullman Timi Ama Sardegna €€€€

Picturesquely located overlooking the bay of Porto Giunco, surrounded by pine forest and a lovely beach, this large hotel has a wide range of services. The rooms are spacious and all have a balcony or terrace with great views. There is also the impressive Thalassotherapy Spa Centre based on the renowned healing properties of the sea (open also to non-residents) and beauty centre. The hotel has three restaurants and three bars. The name "Timi Ama" translates loosely as "fear to love", as local legend says that the sea and its mermaids bewitch all who stay here.

**🔲 169 D1 ⊠ Località Notteri ☎ 070 79791; www.accorhotels.com**

## Stella Maris Hotel €€€

Overlooking Capo Carbonara on the southeastern tip of Sardinia, this hotel has a lovely setting, cradled in the bay of Campulongu. Attractive gardens lead down to the white sandy beach and there's also a freshwater swimming pool. Rooms are traditionally furnished and the best have sea views (supplement). The hotel is 3km (1.5 miles) from the centre of Villasimius.

**🔲 169 D1 ⊠ Località Campulongu ☎ 070 797100; www.stella-maris.com**

## BARÚMINI

### Hotel Su Nuraxi €

A stone's throw from Su Nuraxi, this hotel is simply furnished but has lovely views of the Giara plateau as well as the *nuraghe*. It is a good spot for lolling around in the *lolla* – a

large Sardinian porch – taking in the views across waves of golden wheat fields. The restaurant serves traditional fare from land and sea, including *lumache alla diavola* (devilled snails), *traffiette speck funghi e noci* (pasta with raw ham, mushrooms and nuts) and entrecôte of beef or horse.

**🔲 168 A5 ⊠ Viale Su Nuraxi 6, Strada Provinciale Barúmini–Tuili (immediately after the Nuraghic village) ☎ 070 936 8305, 070 936 8591; www.hotel.sunuraxi.it**

## ISOLA DI SAN PIETRO

### Hotel Riviera €€€

This terracotta-coloured building is a landmark on the harbourfront and is the island's chicest hotel. Under the same management as Le Méridien Chia Laguna (see right), it oozes style and comfort. All 44 rooms are very spacious and individually decorated, complete with luxurious marble bathrooms. There is also an attractive rooftop terrace overlooking the harbour.

**🔲 166 A3 ⊠ Corso Battellieri 26 ☎ 078 185 4101; www.hotelriviera-carloforte.com**

## ISOLA DI SANT'ANTÍOCO

### B&B Gaulos Sant'Antíoco €

A small B&B close to the island's main sights – the Phoenician *tophet*, museum, castle, necropolis and catacombs. Guests can tour these on the bicycles provided by the B&B. Rooms are freshly renovated and comfortable, with en-suite facilities. The hosts have lots of suggestions for hidden beaches and little-known island secrets, such as a sea arch and *nuraghi* to explore.

**🔲 166 B2 ⊠ Via Goceano 45, Sant'Antíoco ☎ 347 049 2487, 347 049 2488; www.gaulosbb.com**

## CHIA (DOMUS DE MARIA)

### Le Méridien Chia Laguna Resort €€€€

Set in the beautiful bay of Chia, just 700m (765 yards) from the

sea, this resort offers elegant accommodation in attractively refurbished hotel rooms, which have spectacular views to the sea, or in family rooms in the Mediterranean garden of Chia Village. The decor is based around soft pastel colours, natural woods and cool tile floors. A regular *trenino* (small train) shuttle service goes back and forth to a beautiful unspoiled bay of white sand dunes. There is a popular miniclub for children, a disco and live music at the new Luna under the stars and a Centro Benessere (beauty centre) and gym as well as several restaurants and swimming pools. Service is exemplary and, although the place is large, there is no feeling of being in a resort complex.

Accommodation is also offered in the Baia Chia Hotel and luxury villas and apartments scattered throughout the resort.

**🔲 167 E1 ⊠ Località Chia, Domus de Maria ☎ 070 92391; www.chialagunaresort.com**

# Where to...
## Eat and Drink

### Prices

Expect to pay per person for a meal, excluding drinks, tax and tip:

€ under €26          €€ €26–€55          €€€ over €55

### CÁGLIARI

#### Dal Corsaro €€€

This is a temple to gastronomy in elegant surroundings. The family-owned restaurant is an institution of the Cágliari culinary scene and attracts gourmets. Service is exemplary and the wine list is long.

➕ 170 C4 ☒ Viale Regina Margherita 28 ☎ 070 664318; www.dalcorsaro.com ⊙ Mon–Sat lunch, dinner; closed mid-Aug for two weeks

#### Dr Ampex €

The genial host doesn't speak English, but you'll immediately feel welcome at his culinary retreat for locals. There is no menu; a prix fixe of €25 brings course after course of delectable starters, a choice of main dish based on the freshest and best market ingredients, plus dessert, wine and *mirto*. The chef breathes new life into traditional Sardinian dishes, for example carpaccio of *bue rossa* (red ox) with slivered artichokes and mushrooms, or pasta with sea urchins, redolent of the Med. You won't find better food or better value on the island.

➕ 170 B5 ☒ Via San Giacomo 35, Villanova ☎ 070 658199 ⊙ Mon–Sat dinner, by reservation

#### Ristorante Italia €–€€

In a narrow street, behind Via Roma, Ristorante Italia has been pleasing locals and visitors since 1921 with traditional specialities served in an unpretentious old-world setting. The menu is rich in fresh seafood, but meat dishes are excellent, especially the roast suckling pig and the carpaccio.

➕ 170 B4 ☒ Via Sardegna 30 ☎ 070 657987 ⊙ Mon–Fri lunch, Sat dinner; closed Aug

### VILLASIMÍUS

#### Ristorante Carbonara €€

This traditional restaurant makes up for its rather lacklustre interior with large portions and very good fish. Choose your delicacy from the platter of fresh offerings and don't be surprised to see lobster antennae waving at you. There's also a good choice of wines.

➕ 169 D1 ☒ Via Umberto I 60 ☎ 070 791270; www.ristorantecarbonaravillasimius.com ⊙ Thu–Tue 12:30–2:30, 8–11

#### Café del Porto €

The only café/bar at the marina and port is good for a snack and admiring the views. *Spaghetti alle vongole e bottarga* (with clams and roe) and *gamberi al Prosecco* (prawns in Prosecco) are typical dishes. There is a WiFi area. Happy hour is from 6:30 to 8:30pm in the restaurant/bar and piano bar, and the new discobar buzzes from 10:30pm during the season.

➕ 169 D1 ☒ Porto di Villasimíus ☎ 070 797 8036; www.cafedelporto.it ⊙ Daily 7am–2am

#### Stella Maris Hotel €€

There are two sea-facing restaurants at this hotel (▶ 59), one inside and the other, alfresco with a veranda, has an especially beautiful location, with the sound of the water lapping and the rustling of the pine trees in the background. Fish is a speciality here, and there is a good wine list.

➕ 169 D1 ☒ Località Campulongu ☎ 070 797100; www.stella-maris.com ⊙ Daily lunch and dinner

## Marina Giò €–€€

North of Villasimius, on a sand road along the beach, this local favourite serves generous portions of dishes that stretch the usual Sardinian repertoire a bit – pork *impanata alla marina giò* is a fork-tender breaded cutlet with cheese and tomato, a dish not found elsewhere. Pizzas are prepared in a wood-fired oven, and ingredients for all dishes are sourced locally, in keeping with the island's traditions (▶ 7). It's right on the beach, with ocean views and a terrace in the summer, when reservations are a good idea.

🖽 169 E3 ☒ Marina di San Giovanni, Muravera ☎ 333 986 0200; www.marinagio.
it ⏲ Tue–Sun 12:30–3, 6–12

### BARÚMINI

## Sa Lolla Albergo Ristorante €€

This restaurant with rooms is in an old, restored country house with magnificent views over the Giara landscape. The pleasant rustic atmosphere is complemented by good food, specializing in seasonal Sardinian and Italian dishes.

🖽 168 A5 ☒ Via Cavour 49 ☎ 070 936 8419; www.wels.it/salolla/ ⏲ Thu–Tue lunch and dinner

### ISOLA DI SAN PIETRO

## Da Nicolò €€€

This famous restaurant has a faithful following. Dine on luscious fish specialities alfresco on the palm-shaded terrace. The selection includes traditional Theabarkina dishes (a local blend of Ligurian, Mediterranean, and North African cuisines), such as *cashca'* (couscous), tuna *bottarga* (roe) and salt-cured tuna fillet.

🖽 166 A3 ☒ Corso Cavour 32, Carloforte ☎ 0781 854048 ⏲ Easter–Sep Tue–Sun lunch and dinner

### ISOLA DI SANT' ANTÍOCO

## Ristorante Renzo e Rita €–€€

Sardinian specialities join a wider Mediterranean mix on the menu of this restaurant owned by the same family for generations. Expect the freshest of seafood, including grilled tuna and swordfish, and only Sardinian wines, a list in which they take justifiable pride. The separate pizzeria prepares more than 40 different pizza toppings.

🖽 166 B2 ☒ Via Nazionale 42, Sant' Antíoco ☎ 0781 800448; www.renzoerita.com ⏲ Summer Thu–Tue 6:30–1am; winter 6–12:30am

### BUGGERRU

## Pizzeria San Nicolò €–€€

This is a restaurant with a view if ever there was one. Fabulous sweeping stretches of white sand are often buffeted with big surf (the Sardinia surf trophy is held here in June). The restaurant specializes in the freshest grilled seafood, but the pastas and meat dishes are worth considering, too.

🖽 166 B4 ☒ Località San Nicolò ☎ 0781 54359; www.ristorantesannicolo.it ⏲ Daily lunch and dinner

### POETTO

## Lo Spinnaker €€€

The first floor terrace restaurant has glorious views of the Golfo degli Angeli. The speciality is fresh fish and seafood and, like its sister restaurant, Dal Corsaro (▶ 60), it is a highly prized venue on the dining circuit. Downstairs there is a much less pricey but very good pizzeria.

🖽 168 B2 ☒ Località Marina Píccola ☎ 070 370295; www.ristorantelospinnaker.it ⏲ May–Sep Tue–Sun lunch and dinner

### CHIA

## Le Dune €

Stop for lunch or a snack in this alfresco bar/café, near the beach. Those in the know opt for the fish or pizzas. Relax in wickerwork chairs on the sand or seek out the shade of the veranda.

🖽 167 E7 ☒ Le Meridien Chia Laguna ☎ 070 9239; www.chialagunaresort.com ⏲ Bar and pizzeria daily 12:30–3, snack bar 3–6; seafood dinners 7–11

# Where to...
## Shop

### CLOTHES

For clothes and boutiques, from Bastione di San Remy in Cágliari, take the **Via Manno** down to Piazza Yenne. **Via Roma** also has some designer shops and the department store **Rinascente** (open Mon–Fri 9–8:30, Sat 9–9, Sun 10–9). The main street, **Carlo Largo Felice**, has some shops and plenty of African traders selling handbags, sunglasses and all kinds of other accessories, some of which may not be what they seem (▶ 152). Nearby, **Sapori di Sardegna** (Vico dei Mille 1, off Via Roma, tel: 070 684 8747; www.saporidisardegna. com) is a little shop crammed full of Sardinian delicacies such as cheese, salamis, wines and *dolci sardi*. It is also a good place to pick up ceramics and other decorously packaged souvenirs.

### CRAFTS AND ANTIQUES

Near the cathedral in Cágliari's Castello district, **Via La Marmora** has a plethora of antiques shops and galleries. The Marina district is also full of artisan shops specializing in craftwork and curios. A good starting point is **ISOLA**, the Institute for Sardinian Handicrafts, which has its headquarters at Via Bacaredda 176. For antiques and bric-a-brac there are markets at **Piazza del Carmine** on the first Sunday of the month, at **Piazza Carlo Alberto** on the second and fourth Sundays and a fleamarket at **Bastione di San Remy** every Sunday except during August.

# Where to...
## Be Entertained

### THEATRE AND MUSIC

The most important theatres in Cágliari are the **Teatro Lirico** (Via Sant'Alenixedda, tel: 070 408 2230; www.teatroliricodicagliari. it) for opera, ballet and classical music; the **Teatro Alfieri** (Via della Pineta 29, tel: 070 301378), staging classical theatre; and the **Exma** complex (Via San Lucifero 71, tel: 070 666399), putting on concerts and recitals. The **Anfiteatro Romano** (tickets from the Teatro Lirico) hosts open-air music, dance and concerts in summer. In the east of the city the **Fiera Campionaria** (Viale Diaz 221) has open-air rock concerts in the summer. There's a free listings magazine available from the tourist office.

### NIGHTLIFE

Late-night bars and cafés in Cágliari include **Caffè degli Spiriti** and, near the Bastione, **San Remy** with live music and DJs. **Jko'** (Via Contivecchi) is the locals' favourite disco, packed from midnight to 5am Thu–Sat, except in summer, when they head for Poetto and the other beaches with nightlife spots.

### FESTIVALS

Sardinia's biggest religious festival is the four-day **Festa di Sant'Efisio** (▶ 40) at the start of May. The statue of Cágliari's patron saint, Efisio, leads a procession to Nora, in commemoration of the saint saving Cágliari from plague.

# Oristano
# and the West

# Getting Your Bearings

Amid forests, fields of wheat, glorious countryside and unpolluted coast, you will experience the true Sardinia. Of the four Sardinian provinces, this is the smallest – and small is beautiful. Prehistoric settlements, *nuraghi* and the evocative Phoenician/Roman site of Thárros are all part of the west's impressive archaeological heritage. Inland, the horse is king, while the coast is awash with lagoons ringed by pink haloes of pretty flamingos.

Oristano and its province form one of the lesser-known areas on the island but, despite that, it is a rewarding one for visitors. This "wild west" horse country is the site of one of Sardinia's most thrilling equestrian festivals. The small city has an excellent collection of archaeology and art in its Antiquarium Arborense which puts into context the nearby Thárros site. The Sínis Peninsula is perfect not only for its historical sites but also for its good beaches and birdlife.

Inland there are many traces of the Nuraghic culture and one of the island's most impressive examples, the Nuraghe Losa. There are citrus trees and silvery olive groves producing the finest virgin olive oil. Prized as the cattle market of the island, you can feast on the best steak – the *bue rosso* – while around the coast there is a bounty of fishy delights, including the prized *bottarga* – "Sardinian caviar" made from mullet roe. And, away from the flat coast, there is the scenic highland of the extinct volcano Monte Ferru with pretty market towns.

**Page 63: La Zona delle Due Colonne, Thárros**

**Below: Santa Maria della Neve, Cúglieri**

# In Three Days

If you're not quite sure where to begin your travels, this itinerary recommends a practical and enjoyable three days exploring Oristano and the west of Sardinia, taking in some of the best places to see using the Getting Your Bearings map on the previous page. For more information see the main entries.

# Day 1

**Morning**
Start in **❶ Oristano** by visiting the Antiquarium Arborense (➤ 68), then drive west on the SS131 to **❺ Marina di Torre Grande** (➤ 74).

**Lunch**
Tuck in at one of the cafés in Marina di Torre Grande.

**Afternoon and Evening**
Drive through the **❸ Sínis Peninsula** (➤ 71; top right), pausing at the Stagno di Cábras, then on to **❻ San Salvatore** (➤ 74–75, 6km/4 miles west of Marina di Torre Grande) and have a drink at the Abraxas Chiosco bar. In the afternoon, visit **❷ Thárros** (above; ➤ 70) at the end of the peninsula – allow a couple of hours for leisurely strolling and try to time it towards sunset when the colours are at their most vibrant. Return to Oristano and stay overnight at the Albergo Duomo (➤ 77).

# Day 2

### Morning
From Oristano drive north on the SS131, the Carlo Felice highway, for 35km (22 miles) to Abbasanta, where you branch left onto the SP15, signposted Santu Lussúrgiu (15km/9 miles). This is a scenic drive among chestnut and olive groves and craggy hills.

### Lunch
Try the Bellavista at Santu Lussúrgiu (Viale Azuni 70, tel: 0783 552045).

### Afternoon
Head north on the minor road signposted Macomér and stop at **9 San Leonardo de Siete Fuéntes** (➤ 76). Take the very scenic, winding SP19 going north and west of Santu Lussúrgiu for 17km (11 miles) to **8 Cúglieri** (➤ 75–76). Stay overnight at Santa Caterina di Pittinuri in Hotel La Baja (➤ 78).

# Day 3

### Morning
Take the SS292 from Cúglieri north to Tresnuraghes and onto Suni. Bear right going east on the SS129 bis to Macomér and then south on the Carlo Felice highway towards Abbasanta, turning off to the right just before onto the SS131 to Ghilarza.

### Afternoon
Visit the **4 Nuraghe Losa** in Abbasanta (➤ 72–73). Take the SS313 minor road to **10 Fordongiánus** (➤ 76) and check out the Terme Romane (Roman Baths, right), then head west on the SS388, following the River Tirso for 28km (17 miles), back to Oristano.

# ❶ Oristano

"*Città della ceramica*" (City of Ceramics) is the sign that welcomes you to Oristano. It is also the site of the colourful Sa Sartiglia festival during Carnival. But perhaps most striking is the city's location itself, lying at the northern end of the fertile Campidano plain, surrounded by lagoons and only 5km (3 miles) from the sea.

Evidence of human habitation in this area dates right back to the sixth millennium BC before the Nuraghic civilization began to spread. By the ninth century BC the first Phoenician merchants landed at Thárros, on the coast of Sínis, the ancestor of Oristano. Thárros was later abandoned to escape the increasingly frequent raids by the Moors. As the local expression goes, "*Portant de Tharros sa perda a carros*" ("They're bringing cartloads of stones from Tharros") – to build the new town, originally named Aristanis, meaning "between the ponds".

Oristano reached a new zenith during the Middle Ages when the whole island, with the sole exceptions of Cágliari and Alghero, was under Oristano's control. In the ensuing struggle between Pisans and Catalans, the town sided with the Catalans and centuries of economic neglect followed. However, the town is now reviving its fortunes and is Sardinia's fourth provincial capital.

The **Piazza Roma** is at the heart of town with its medieval tower, Torre di Mariano II, also known as San Cristoforo. The tower is a unique remnant of the city walls, to which it was joined and which were destroyed at the end of the 19th century.

### Archaeological Museum

The top sight is the town's **Antiquarium Arborense**, just southeast of Piazza Roma. This is home to one of the island's top archaeological collections, with displays spanning prehistoric, Nuraghic, Phoenician and Roman treasures. On the ground floor a **fourth-century BC lion** from Thárros (➤ 70) greets you. There are **tiny ivory dice**, a green jasper scarab dating from the sixth century BC and numerous figurines and **ceramics**. There are masks, too, recovered from Thárros, to keep the evil eye at bay – "apotropaic" masks put in beside the dead in Punic times to cast away evil spirits. Some of the grimacing faces are enough to scare the life out of you. There are also human bones (fifth to first century BC) and terracotta urns with the remains of stillborn babies from fourth-century Thárros.

On the first floor you can see a **reconstruction of Roman Thárros** as it probably appeared in the fourth century AD.

The onion-domed tower of the Duomo stands out above the houses of Oristano

## Duomo

The Duomo (cathedral) is the largest in Sardinia and is devoted to Santa Maria Assunta. Although founded in the 12th century, its current baroque style is the result of an 18th-century reconstruction. However, inside are the remaining Gothic vestiges of the groin-vaulted **Rimedio Chapel** in the right transept. Look out, too, for the 14th-century *Annunciation* by Nino Pisano and fragments of a **medieval marble pulpit** depicting Daniel in the Lions' Den. The onion-domed campanile is a symbol of the Oristano skyline.

### TAKING A BREAK

Enjoy a glass or two of Oristano's famous Vernaccia dessert wine.

➕ 162 C3

**Antiquarium Arborense**
✉ Piazzetta Corrias
☎ 0783 791262  🕐 Daily 9–2, 3–8  💰 Moderate

**Duomo**
✉ Piazza Duomo
🕐 Apr–Oct daily 8–1, 4–7; Nov–Mar 7–1, 3–6:30

---

### ORISTANO: INSIDE INFO

**Top tip** Oristano itself is not worth a long linger, but it is well positioned as a jumping-off point for the local sights. The exception to this is the **Sa Sartiglia** during Carnival (➤ 16, 40), when it is certainly worth the detour.

# ② Thárros

The Phoenicians chose this site because of its harbour, but they could not have failed to appreciate its beauty, on a high point sloping down to the sea. Today's picture-postcard scene includes a Spanish watchtower overlooking the foundations of the Roman city, with a pair of tall columns as a focal point.

The extensive Roman ruins at Thárros

Lying 20km (12 miles) west of Oristano, this is one of the island's **top archaeological sites**. It wasn't until 1956 that excavations began in earnest to reveal this prosperous Phoenician port dating back to 730BC. Although most of what is now visible belongs to the Roman period, there are still remnants of the Phoenician city in a temple with Doric half-columns and, north of the main site, a *tophet*, or children's burial ground.

The Roman city had the usual shops, taverns, baths and amphitheatre. At the northern end you will find a relatively modest second to third century AD example of this, partially occupying the area of the *tophet*. Gladiatorial and wild beast contests were staged here for the delight of up to 8,000 people during the Roman era. Nowadays, there are **open-air performances** on a makeshift stage by the sea in high season. Sunset at Thárros is a magical experience.

Thárros' **Torre di San Giovanni** (9am–sunset) can be climbed for spectacular views – depending on wind conditions. Not for nothing is Thárros known as being on the windy peninsula.

➕ 162 B3 ☎ 0783 397306 🕐 Apr–Oct daily 9–1, 4–8; Nov–Mar 10–1, 3–7
🕐 Daily till sunset in high season. Performances usually begin at 9:30pm
💶 Moderate (includes Museo Cívico in Cábras)

# ③ Sínis Peninsula

This low-lying peninsula west of Oristano is a watery wonderland full of large lagoons, regularly visited by migrating birds and pretty pink flamingos.

Sínis Peninsula is famous, too, for the coracle-style *fassoni* boats used by the local fishermen to catch the bounty of these waters. While they net the mullet and eel, the peace is broken only by the honking of the ruddy shelduck, indigenous to this lagoon but extinct in mainland Italy. Birds flock to these lagoons from all over Africa and Europe. You should be able to see flamingos at many times of the year but they arrive in their thousands in the autumn at the **Stagno di Mistras**, west of Oristano.

The peninsula's main town, **Cábras**, lies languidly on the eastern side of its eponymous lagoon – Stagno di Cábras – which separates the Sínis from the rest of Sardinia. This huge lagoon covers 2,000ha (5,000 acres) and is one of Europe's most fascinating ecological wetlands. The sleepy fishing town's great claim to fame is as the headquarters of Sardinia's mullet fishing, used in the local delicacy *bottarga* (mullet roe).

The only sight of note is the **Museo Cívico**, whose entrance fee is included in the ticket to Thárros. This excellent small museum showcases finds from Thárros, such as urns containing the bones of animals and children. It also displays discoveries made in the late 1990s at Cuccuru S'Arrius, about 4km (2 miles) away. This was a necropolis carbon-dated to the middle neolithic period (fourth millennium BC) – the oldest hypogeum burials discovered on the island.

✚ 162 B3

**Cábras is the main town on the Sínis Peninsula**

**Museo Cívico**
✉ Via Thárros 121, Cábras ☎ 0783 290636 🕐 Apr–Oct daily 9–1, 4–8; Nov–Mar 9–1, 3–7 💶 Inexpensive

# 4 Nuraghe Losa

Just a couple of miles west of the Carlo Felice highway (SS131), this huge megalithic monument looms into view. It is one of Sardinia's most important and best-preserved monuments of the Nuraghic civilization.

Encircled by two large walls – the inner one with small towers – it is built of great basalt blocks and is estimated to be more than 3,500 years old. Easily accessible, this symbol of silence lies in splendid isolation on a grassy site, but within view of the main road.

**Nuraghe Losa is a superb monument**

## The Construction

The *nuraghe* has a truncated cone or beehive shape, built in the distinctive Cyclopean style, which used no mortar – nor indeed any other binding material – but was erected entirely by piling up huge blocks. The central tower, 13m (43 feet) high and 12.5m (41 feet) wide, originally had three floors and, almost certainly, a corbelled top, long since destroyed.

A narrow stone corridor gives access to two of the original three floors of the topless central tower and several ancillary buildings dotted around the site. The tall conical interior is illuminated by sunken lighting and the walls are peppered with niches and alcoves. Around it there are other later

## NURAGHE LOSA: INSIDE INFO

**Hidden gem** Ghilarza, close to Abbasanta, was the boyhood home of Antonio Gramsci, the celebrated Marxist writer, politician and philosopher (1891–1937). His small home in the centre is the **Casa Museo di Antonio Gramsci** (tel: 0785 54164; summer Fri–Sun 10–1, 4–7; winter 3:30–6:30, but not reliable; admission free).

towers, enclosed in an imposing triangular curtain and surrounded and fortified by defensive walls with towers and arrow-slits estimated to date to around the seventh century BC. Winding stone steps lead up to a terrace from where there are splendid views over the high plain and, to the east, as far as Gennargentu on a good visibility day.

### Successive Settlements

As always, the exact origins and functions of these monuments are shrouded in the mists of time. Today there is evidence of an **unexcavated prehistoric village** around the perimeter wall and, inside the main entrance to the site, cinerary urns from the first to second century AD. It is probable that in the post-Nuraghic phase the Phoenicians, Romans and possibly also Byzantines took it over as a fortress. What is known is that the whole "village" was continuously occupied from its middle Bronze Age origins to the seventh century AD. This peaceful, yet eerie, site is the perfect place to let your imagination roam.

**An interior view of the nuraghe**

There is a little museum here with a few artefacts, such as pottery and vases, which were found within the area, but the major finds are in Cágliari's Archaeological Museum (➤ 47). Also in the museum are maps showing the locations of other *nuraghi* and ancient sites.

### TAKING A BREAK

Have lunch in Ghilarza at **Al Marchi**, near Antonio Gramsci's house, or enjoy a picnic by the nearby Lago Omodeo – Italy's largest artificial lake.

✚ 163 D4 ⊠ Parco Archeológico Nuraghe Losa, Abbasanta (about 30km/20 miles northeast of Oristano) ☎ 0785 52302; www.nuraghelosa. net ⊙ Daily 9–5; till 7pm in summer ▥ Moderate. Buy an entry ticket at the small museum/ticket office or at the adjoining café

# At Your Leisure

## 5 Marina di Torre Grande

Named after the Aragonese watchtower that stands sentinel over it, this is the most majestic of all towers erected by the Spanish, built at the end of the 16th century to protect the Sardinian coasts from pirates. The pine- and palm-fronted esplanade faces a wide beach of fine blonde sand, over 1km (0.5 miles) long and especially child-friendly as it shelves gradually into the sea.

Parasols and loungers on the beach are for hire at around €10 each. The beach is also well known on the windsurfing circuit, and you can rent equipment for around €15 an hour. If you prefer to watch others carving creamy wakes across the water, the esplanade is a good spot to linger in one of the many bars and cafés that line the shore. By night the resort really buzzes after the obligatory *passeggiata* along the Lungomare Eleonora d'Arborea. Out of season the whole resort is deserted with the melancholy air of a ghost town.

A little farther south on the Golf of Oristano is the Spiaggia di San Giovanni di Sínis. More exposed, this is a good spot for surf, clean, deep sea and fine, white sand.

🔒 162 B3

## 6 San Salvatore

Off the Thárros road and 6km (4 miles) west of Marina di Torre Grande another world awaits. Reminiscent of a "spaghetti western" film set, San Salvatore has a bar, shuttered houses piled together and swirling dust. In the 1960s the Coronca Company transformed part of it into a Mexican village for a less than famous film, *Giarrettiera Colt*, but the place is known today for the Barefoot Race (Corsa degli Scalzi).

The festival (➤ 40) is centred around the sanctuary of San Salvatore – one of Sardinia's *chiese novenari*, churches open for only nine days a year. The climax is the re-enactment of the rescue of the statue of San Salvatore from the Moors. Hundreds of young men in shorts and white shirts make the 8km (5-mile) dash, barefoot, from Cábras to San Salvatore at dawn on the first Saturday of September, and back again the next day. The idea is that by pounding the ground barefoot the earth will be stirred and fertility restored.

The small sixth-century Byzantine church of San Giovanni di Sínis, near San Salvatore, is one of the oldest in Sardinia, with a cupola ceiling and barrel-vaulting. Almost opposite

**Terrace tables at a beachfront café, Marina di Torre Grande**

A quiet street in San Salvatore, scene of the annual Barefoot Race

is the Visitor Center of the Marine Protected Area, from which you can join fishing excursions using historic style boats.

🔢 162 B3  ☎ Fishing excursions 0783 371006; www.areamarinasinis.it

## 7 Monte Ferru Market Towns

North of Oristano the SS292 winds up to the rugged triangle of Monte Ferru (Iron Mountain). The eight communes that comprise the Communità Montana are all characterized by the surrounding densely forested highland studded with gnarled cork oaks, where mouflon and deer roam. The huge red ox (*bue rosso*), prized for its strength and meat, grazes here.

Bonarcado's main street climbs steeply past stone houses to the imposing Romanesque Chiesa di Santa Maria. Next to it is a small Byzantine sanctuary built over the remains of a Roman bath, of which one pool remains.

At the junction of Riola Sardo bear right, to Seneghe. This is the region for Sardinia's finest olive oil. To pick up some bottles and other specialities of the area visit L'Enogastronomia del Montiferru (➤ 80).

🔢 162 C4

A detail of the painted dome of the Chiesa di San Sebastiano in Seneghe

**L'Enogastronomia del Montiferru**
✉ Corso Umberto 141/b  ☎ 0783 54450
🕐 Mon–Fri 8:30–1, 3:30–7

## 8 Cúglieri and Santa Maria della Neve

From San Leonardo turn back south and go west for Cúglieri. Halfway up the slopes of Monte Ferru, this important agricultural town is, along with Seneghe, the leading producer of excellent olive oil. The silver dome of the 15th-century Santa Maria della Neve is visible from miles around. From the basilica's churchyard there

**San Leonardo di Siete Fuéntes, where seven springs deliver mineral waters**

rock, was built in the 12th century by the Knights of St John of Jerusalem. They once ran a hospital next door, where Guelfo, son of Count Ugolino della Gherardesca, died in 1292 after being wounded by the Pisans. He is buried here.

Just to the south, Santu Lussúrgiu is a medieval village nestling inside Sardinia's largest extinct volcano. Protected by Mediterranean oak forests, it is refreshingly cool in the summer with lovely views.

✚ 162 C5

### 🔟 Fordongiánus and Thermal Baths

South of Lake Omodeo is the spa town of Fordongiánus. The Romans set up their spa here on the banks of the River Tirso, and it's still possible to visit the first century AD bath complex. The water that gushes up is a scalding 54°C (129°F), and clouds of steam rise from the river. Outside this area is a hot spring still used by locals for washing clothes.

The town is bathed in a russet glow from the local red trachyte stone, a good example of which is the 16th-century Casa Aragonese. Here there are frequent exhibitions of sculpture carved out of the fiery stone, and an annual competition is held in the town in high season.

Outside town, on SS388 toward Oristano, the small monastery of San Lussorio was built in the early 11th century on an older structure that is now in the process of excavation.

✚ 163 D3

are sublime views of the coast, as far as the cliffs of Porto Conte near Alghero on a clear day. The area has several *nuraghi, domus de janus* and *tombe dei giganti*.

✚ 162 C5

### 🟢 San Leonardo de Siete Fuéntes

True to its name, there are seven springs in this pretty woodland setting and seven taps from which to imbibe the mineral waters. They have a diuretic effect and some are mildly radioactive, but supposedly have great healing powers.

The Romanesque Chiesa di San Leonardo, hewn out of dark trachyte

**Bagni Termali**
⏰ Summer Mon–Sat 8–10, 2:30–6:30; winter 8–10, 2:30–4:30  💰 Moderate

**Terme Romane**
☎ 0783 60157  ⏰ Summer daily 9–1, 3–7; winter 9–1, 2:30–5  💰 Moderate

**Casa Aragonese**
⏰ Apr–Sep Tue–Sun 9:30–1, 3–7:30; Oct–Mar 9:30–1, 3–5:30  💰 Moderate

# Where to...
## Stay

### Prices
Expect to pay per double room, per night:
€ under €90   €€ €90–€155
€€€ €155–€250   €€€€ over €250

### ORISTANO

#### Albergo Duomo €–€€
As its name suggests, this 17th-century building is in the old centre in front of the Duomo. There are 10 spacious, bright rooms, the best of which sit around the courtyard. Traditional Sardinian decorations with local embroidery predominate. There is a good restaurant and bar.
➕ 162 C3 ✉ Via Vittorio Emanuele 34
☎ 0783 778061; www.hotelduomo.net

#### Mistral 2 €€
This modern hotel is right in the centre of town with 132 functional, yet comfortable rooms, and is popular for congresses. Facilities include internet access, a swimming pool and an attractive restaurant.
➕ 162 C3 ✉ Via XX Settembre 34
☎ 0783 210389; www.hotel-mistral.it

### SINIS PENINSULA

#### Agriturismo Su Lau €
A warm welcome awaits in this peaceful rural retreat. There are six very pleasant, comfortable rooms set amid fruit orchards. Dinner in the farmhouse, prepared with fresh seasonal produce, is available by prior booking.
➕ 162 B3 ✉ Via Luigino Bellu 24, Riola Sardo ☎ 0783 410897; www.tribu.it/sulau

#### Hotel Lucrezia €€
A few miles from the coast, and northwest of Oristano, this small historic hotel is situated at the heart of the village. The inner garden has the traditional wine cellar, well and bread oven surrounded by centuries-old trees. The seven rooms are pleasingly decorated with traditional Sardinian furnishings coupled with all modern facilities, including internet connection.
➕ 162 B3 ✉ Via Roma 14a, Riola Sardo
☎ 0783 412078; www.hotellucrezia.it

#### Sa Pedrera €–€€
Lying about 8km (5 miles) out of Cabras, en route to San Giovanni di Sinis, this stone *casa colonide campidanese*, or typical Sardinian hacienda-style hotel, is an oasis of cool. Rooms are simply but comfortably furnished and surrounded by attractive gardens. Excellent beaches are nearby.
➕ 162 B3 ✉ SP Cabras–S Giovanni di Sinis Km 7.5 ☎ 0783 370040; www.sapedrera.it

#### Spinnaker €–€€
Set among pine trees on the seashore, this well-equipped campsite also has comfortable bungalows – some with kitchens. As well as a private beach, there is a swimming pool, and pizzeria, laundry, bathrooms and shop.
➕ 162 B3 ✉ Strada Torre Grande
Pontile–Oristano ☎ 0783 22074;
www.campingspinnaker.com

### NURAGHE LOSA

#### Mandra Edera Farm €€
Once purely an *agriturismo* restaurant, now a hotel, Mandera Edera was established in 2004. Guests sit together at large refectory-style tables for meals with open-plan kitchen. There are Anglo-Arab-Sardo horses to ride and also offroad excursions from the farm. The accommodation comprises four double rooms plus

eight suites/huts, which have a hydro-massage shower.

163 D4 Via Dante 20, Abbasanta 0785 8902222; www.mandraedera.com

## Sa Mola €€

Attached bungalows look out upon manicured lawns and gardens, although from the front entrance Sa Mola appears to be a patrician town house. Nicely furnished rooms are quiet, even when the popular restaurant is filled. Bonarcado is a very attractive town, perfectly placed for exploring Nuraghe Losa, Oristano and the mountain towns, and the hotel is easy to find by car from the Paulilatino road.

162 C4 Via Giardini, Bonarcado 0783 56588; www.samola.it

## SANTU LUSSÚRGIU

### Antica Dimora del Gruccione €–€€

This lovely 17th-century mansion is Spanish in design and filled with antiques. Owner Gabriella Belloni named it after the *gruccione*, a bird that migrates in the summer to Sardinia from the tropics. Every time that Gabriella returned to Santu Lussúrgiu for the summer season to visit her grandparents' house, the *gruccione* was there. This is an *albergo diffuso*, consisting of a main mansion and several other buildings in the neighbourhood. All rooms are individually decorated, some with a colour theme such as "Camera Rossa" (red) or "Suite Limone" (yellow). There is also a very good restaurant.

162 C5 Via Michele Obinu 31 0783 552035; www.anticadimora.com

## CÚGLIERI

### Hotel La Baja €€–€€€

This four-star hotel is near the Sinis Peninsula at the foot of Monte Ferru, around 20km (12 miles) from Oristano. Nearly all of the 29 rooms have balconies, and the swimming pool and restaurant terrace overlook the sea. 162 C5 Via Scirocco 20, Santa Caterina di Pittinuri 0785 389149; www.hotellabaja.it

### Hotel Desogos €

Set in the heart of Cúglieri's old town, this a convenient stopping-off point while exploring the area. The small hotel is comfortable but plainly furnished and rooms are available with or without bathrooms en suite. The restaurant is very good indeed and attracts a lot of locals. This *ristorante/albergo* ("restaurant with rooms") is family run and is very good value for money.

162 C5 Vico Cugia 6 (off the main Via Cugia one-way street through the old town), Cúglieri 0785 39660

## FORDONGIÁNUS

### Sardegna Grand Hotel Terme €€€

This modern spa hotel has comfortable air-conditioned rooms with balconies. There are many different treatments on offer for an extra cost, including Ayurvedic massage, mudpacks, reflexology and bathing in the mineral waters. The hotel lies on the other side of the river from the Terme Romane.

163 D3 Strada Provinciale 48, n.1 0783 605016; www.termesardegna.it

## LAKE OMODEO

### Funtana Lidone €€

On the SP31, northeast of Oristano near Lago Omodeo, this three-star property is also an ecological tourist centre. Set in the midst of parkland, its traditional farmhouse-style buildings are of local stone with tiled floors. There are 12 bedrooms furnished in natural fabrics which are eco-friendly but still offer all the usual comforts such as telephone, TV, internet and en suite facilities. The restaurant specializes in traditional Sardinian recipes from the area using local produce.

163 E4 Via Giovanni XXIII, Neoneli 0783 67603, 320 539 7876; www.funtanalidone.com

# Where to...
## Eat and Drink

**Prices**

Expect to pay per person for a meal, excluding drinks, tax and tip:

€ under €26          €€ €26–€55          €€€ over €55

## ORISTANO

### Cocco & Dessì €€

Innovative cuisine served in several dining spaces, including a gazebo, in this fashionable restaurant. The menu includes seasonal specialities. Pizzas are available in the evening.

➕ 162 C3 ⊠ Via Tirso 31 ☎ 0783 300720; www.ristorantecoccodessi.com ⓦ Tue–Sun lunch and dinner; closed Sun eve and three weeks in Jan

### Craf €€

The welcoming vaulted dining room was a 17th-century granary. The varied menu, relying on seasonal produce, has some tasty offerings for meat- and fish-eaters. Soup, such as *panne frattau*, made with Sardinian bread, is a meal in itself.

➕ 162 C3 ⊠ Via de Castro 34 ☎ 078 370669 ⓦ Mon–Sat lunch and dinner

### Il Faro €€–€€€

This class act, offers traditional Sardinian specialities in an atmospheric, yet relaxed restaurant. Seasonal dishes predominate and there is a good wine list with emphasis on local and regional offerings. The service is excellent.

➕ 162 C3 ⊠ Via Bellini 25 ☎ 0783 70002; www.il-faro.eu ⓦ Mon–Sat 12:45–2:45, 8–10; closed Sun and third week of Dec to third week of Jan

## SINIS PENINSULA

### Il Caminetto €€

Very popular with both locals and tourists, the menu here specializes in fish and seafood. Mullet features, not just *bottarga* (roe) but also *sa merca* (salted and cooked in herbs) or *affumicato* (smoked).

➕ 162 B3 ⊠ Via Cesare Battisti 8, Cábras ☎ 0783 391139; www.hotelvillacanu.com ⓦ Tue–Sun lunch and dinner

### Sa Funtà €€

This restaurant has a marine flavour, with wooden tables and fishing tackle. The specialities, too, are authentically Sardinian. Fishy delights include *burrida* (marinated dogfish), *anguilla con carciofi* (eel with artichokes) and *seppitte alla vernaccia* (cuttlefish in white wine).

➕ 162 B3 ⊠ Via Garibaldi 25, Cábras ☎ 0783 290685 ⓦ Mon–Sat lunch and dinner; closed mid-Dec to Feb

## BONARCADO

### Sa Mola €–€€

As you might expect from Sardinia's passion for locally produced foods, this excellent restaurant is part of the Slow Food movement. Find local *cinghiale* (wild boar) served as a carpaccio, and local beef prepared with wild mushrooms and Sardinian wine. The separate pizzeria is also outstanding.

➕ 162 C4 ⊠ Via Giardini ☎ 0783 56588; www.samola.it ⓦ Mon–Sat lunch and dinner, pizzeria also Sun dinner

## MONTE FERRU

### Al Bue Rosso €€

The Red Ox specializes in the local *bue rosso* beef, prized by gourmets. Other local delicacies on the menu include *casiz olu* (cow's cheese). Reserving ahead is advised.

➕ 162 C4 ⊠ Piazzale Montiferru 3/4, Seneghe ☎ 0783 54384 ⓦ Apr–Oct Tue–Sun lunch and dinner; Nov–Mar Tue, Wed closed dinner

# Where to...
# Shop

In **Oristano** there are morning markets in **Via Mazzini** and **Via Costa** (Mon–Sat) and on the first Saturday of the month there's an antiques and bric-a-brac market in **Piazza Eleonora**. The area is renowned for its white Vernaccia wine, and the **Cantina Sociale della Vernaccia** is at Via Oristano 149, Rimedio (tel: 0783 33155; www.vinovernaccia.com; Mon–Fri 8–1, 3:30–6). Local winegrowers bring their grapes here to be crushed and you can buy from the source in the cantina shop. **ISOLA**, which showcases traditional handicrafts, is on Piazza Eleonora 18 (tel: 0783 779025).

In **Seneghe** visit **Macelleria il Bue Rosso** at Vicolo Angioy 4 (tel: 078 354171; Tue–Sat; closed Wed pm) for *bue rosso* steak. The **Enogastronomia del Montiferru** at Corso Umberto 141/b (tel: 078 354450) showcases food and wine products of the region, including the prestigious olive oil and mountain honey.

In **Cabras**, the local speciality is dried grey mullet roe *bottarga*, known as Sardinian caviar, which is sold widely. This is a good place to stock up on Vernaccia wine.

**Santu Lussurgiu** is famous for its handicrafts, especially knives, pruning hooks and traditional iron and wood crafts. It is also a town devoted to horsemanship, so many shops stock saddles and other horsey accoutrements.

The citrus fruit oasis of **Milis** produces Sardinia's best oranges for 10 months of the year. There is also a wine show in early November.

# Where to...
# Be Entertained

## TOURS AND EXCURSIONS

There are many tours, excursions and horseback riding opportunities in the area. For more details contact the tourist information centre at Piazza Eleonora d'Arborea 19 (tel: 0783 36831; www.inforistano.it; Mon–Fri 8–2, 4–7).

## NIGHTLIFE

For nightlife, **Oristano** is the best bet, with a good selection of bars that stay open late. Among the top spots is the stylish **Lola Mundo** café (Piazzetta Corrias 14), which is open until 1am Friday and Saturday and until 9 on other weekdays. On Via Ghilarza there are clubs that are open in winter only, such as **Ovest** (Via Ghilarza 5), which is open on Friday and Saturday from 11pm. The **Lux Club** (www.luxclub.it) often has Caribbean and Latin sounds and sometimes live bands, while next door at No 9 the **Neo-geo** has more chart and techno music, also with occasional live bands, open Fridays and Saturdays only.

The whole town explodes into life during the **Sa Sartiglia** festival (▶ 16, 40) of costumes and horsemanship. Also in Oristano, **Teatro Garau** (Via Parpaglia; tel: 0783 78886) is the venue for dance and music performances, both popular and classical.

On the coast at **Marina di Torre Grande**, bars and clubs line the esplanade in summer, but out of season it becomes rather like a ghost town.

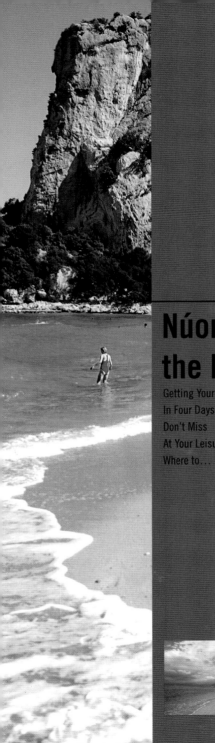

# Núoro and the East

# Getting Your Bearings

In the heart of the island rise the highest mountains of the Gennargentu. Known today as the Barbágia, this part of Sardinia was never conquered by invaders. This is a land of shepherds, pastoral farming, dramatic scenery and tradition, where villages are few and far between. It also has a wildly beautiful coastline indented with idyllic coves, grottoes and caves, and glorious beaches of pristine white sand.

Núoro, although not overly endowed with sights, is well worth scratching the surface of to discover some of the island's best museums. It is also a good base for visiting the mural town of Orgosolo and the carnival town, Mamoiada. Nearby, too, is Monte Ortobene and the dramatic range of the Gennargentu. Today the image of mountain bandits is still bolstered by some fanciful tourist literature, but, in reality, new roads and communications have tamed those antisocial scenarios, although sheep rustling continues and doubtless vendettas are still waged, but quietly.

To the east lies the spectacular, undeveloped coastline of the Golfo di Orosei. Near Dorgali, the Grotta di Ispinigoli has Europe's tallest stalagmite, and on the coast, the Grotta del Bue Marino is to Sardinia what the Blue Grotto is to Capri. Cala Gonone on the coast is spectacularly set against an amphitheatre of forested mountains and, although now a popular resort, still has a villagey, laid-back atmosphere. From here there are excellent hiking and climbing excursions, including the Gola Su Gorruppu Gorge and Tiscali, the Nuraghic village, concealed in a mountain chasm.

**Page 81: Cala di Luna, near Cala Gonone, Golfo di Orosei**

**Below: The Monti del Gennargentu range**

# In Four Days

**If you're not quite sure where to begin your travels, this itinerary recommends a practical and enjoyable four days exploring Núoro and the East, taking in some of the best places to see using the Getting Your Bearings map on the previous page. For more information see the main entries.**

## Day 1

### Morning
Travel to – or wake up in – **1** Núoro (➤ 86–87). Visit the tourist office and then head to the old part of town and visit the Museo Deleddiano. Walk to the Corso Garibaldi and have a coffee at Bar Majore. Just to the east is the Piazza Santa Maria della Neve, where you can visit the eponymous cathedral.

### Lunch
Have lunch at Il Rifugio (➤ 96).

### Afternoon
Walk south to the outstanding Museo della Vita e delle Tradizioni Sarde (left) – where you can easily spend at least an hour, depending on how many exhibits are open. In the late afternoon, as the sun loses its intensity, drive (or go by public transport) to **4** Monte Ortobene (➤ 92) for splendid views across the countryside. Return to Núoro for dinner and the night.

## Day 2

### Morning
Set off for the **3** Golfo di Orosei (➤ 90–91). Arrive at Restaurant Ispinigoli (below entrance to the Grotta) and have a coffee while waiting for tours on the hour. Visit the **6** Grotta di Ispinigoli (➤ 93; top right).

### Lunch
Have lunch at Dorgali's Ristorante Albergo Sant'Elene (➤ 96).

### Afternoon and Evening
Arrive at Cala Gonone (right). Relax on the beach or take a boat trip to the Grotta del Bue Marino (➤ 90–91), visiting other beaches en route. Spend the night at Cala Gonone.

# Day 3

### Morning
Take an all-day excursion to **2 Tiscali** (➤ 88) or to **9 Gola Su Gorruppu** (➤ 93–94) from Cala Gonone. Lunch is included in the excursions, or pack a picnic.

### Evening
Have dinner at Ristorante Al Porto (at the Hotel Pop; ➤ 96).

# Day 4

### Morning
Drive via the **10 Gennargentu** (➤ 94) to **8 Orgosolo** (➤ 93). Stroll around the "town of murals".

### Lunch
Stop for lunch at Ai Monti del Gennargentu (➤ 97; 5km/3 miles outside Orgosolo going south out of town, uphill towards Montes).

### Afternoon
Visit **7 Mamoiada** (➤ 93) and take in the Museo delle Maschere Mediterranee before returning to Núoro.

# ❶ Núoro

**Núoro is at the heartland of Sardinia's traditions and, although not especially aesthetically pleasing, gave birth to distinguished literary sons and daughters whose lives have been indelibly marked by this overgrown mountain village of granite. D H Lawrence followed up his remark that there was nothing to see in Núoro by saying "I am not Baedeker". But then, he wasn't a Nobel Prize winner like writer Grazia Deledda either.**

The old part of town in the northeast spreads around Piazza San Giovanni and Corso Garibaldi. On the northern fringes is the **Museo Deleddiano**, the birthplace and home of Grazia Deledda (1871–1936). She was the first Italian woman to win the Nobel Prize for Literature (1926) and is one of Italy's most important early 20th-century "realist" writers. Her writings describe life on her native island with depth and sympathy and deal with human problems in general. She lived here for 29 years and the museum gives an insight into life in a Nuorese house, together with her memorabilia, including first editions, press clippings and her old photos.

## Cathedral

On **Piazza Santa Maria della Neve** is Núoro's large neoclassical cathedral. Completed in 1854, it is more quantitative than qualitative. But inside, among the mainly 20th-century paintings, the *Disputa de Gesù Fra i Dottori (Jesus' Dispute in the Temple)* is a 17th-century canvas attributed to the Neapolitan studio of Luca Giordano. Behind the cathedral there are spectacular views out across the valley to Monte Ortobene.

## NÚORO: INSIDE INFO

**In more depth** Núoro's famous writers include poet **Sebastiano Satta** (1867–1914) and novelist **Salvatore Satta** (1902–75) – no relation. The latter chronicled the island's colourful life in *Il Giorno del Giudizio (The Day of Judgement)*.

### Museum of Sardinian Life

South of the Duomo is the most famous attraction in Núoro – the **Museo della Vita e delle Tradizioni Sarde** – often referred to simply as the "Museo del Costume". There are 7,000 items here, but they may not all be on display, since the museum is undergoing major reorganization. The breathtaking collection of **traditional costumes** will be, however, and they are the highlight, showing the vast variety in styles and the amazingly sophisticated hand needlework produced all across the island. Gorgeous **jewellery** ranges from intricate silver filigree to wild boar tusks. Displays of decorative arts surround the costumes. The other highlight certain to be on view is the display on the

*mamuthones* and other masked and costumed participants in the region's carnival celebrations (➤ 12, 93).

**Above: The facade of Duomo Santa Maria della Neve**

**Right: A display in the Museum of Sardinian Life**

**Left: Corso Garibaldi**

### TAKING A BREAK

Have a coffee at the **Bar Majore** (➤ 96), which is Núoro's oldest and most opulent café.

➕ 164 C4

**Museo Deleddiano**
✉ Via Grazia Deledda 53  ☎ 0784 258088  🕐 Mid-Jun to Sep Tue–Sat 9–8, Sun 9–1; Oct to mid-Jun Tue–Sun 9–1, 3–7  💰 Moderate

**Duomo Santa Maria della Neve**
✉ Piazza Santa Maria della Neve  🕐 Daily 8–1, 4–7

**Museo della Vita e delle Tradizioni Sarde**
✉ Via A Mereu 56  ☎ 0784 257035  🕐 Mid-Jun to Sep daily 9–8; Oct to mid-Jun 9–1, 3–7  💰 Inexpensive

# ② Tiscali Villaggio Nuragico

Renato Soru, founder of the Italian internet service provider Tiscali, named his company after a huge silent cave on the top of a mountain in the centre of his native Sardinia, in which ancient islanders used to hide from their enemies. The inaugural advertising slogan was "Tiscali. From a land of silence comes a new way of communication."

In the heart of the Supramonte, Tiscali houses the remains of a village dating back to the final Nuraghic period. Nearby, the Gola Su Gorruppu is one of the deepest and most dramatic canyons in Europe.

**Sa Sedda 'e Sos Carros is still under excavation**

**Monte Tiscali** stands at 515m (1,690 feet) and within it is a wide crater concealing the Nuraghic village – originally a site of more than 60 round dwellings, most now ruined. It is thought that it was built in late Nuraghic times to escape the Roman domination, for which this was a perfect spot given the rugged terrain and high crater walls. The site continued to be inhabited into medieval times, but was only discovered in the 19th century and is still under excavation. It is a very atmospheric place, buried in the mountain with stalactites and trees inside and remnants of the *nuraghi* within.

### Trek to Tiscali

It's best to take a guide to do this full-day trek, organized through the tourist information office in Oliena (➤ 92). However, should you wish to undertake it on your own (and risk not finding the signs) the best starting point is from the natural spring at Sorgente Su Gologone next to the Hotel Su Gologone, just off the Oliena–Dorgali road.

From the spring there is a signpost for the Valle di Lanaittu, a track that is mainly unasphalted so best tackled in a 4x4 vehicle or on foot. After about 6km (4 miles), follow the signpost to the right for Grotta Sa Oche (Cave of the Voice). Just north of here is the Nuraghic site of **Sa Sedda 'e Sos Carros** with the remains of 150 *nuraghi* (still under excavation). Walk along the main track past the Grotta Sa Oche keeping left (southwest) to climb up a steep dirt track. Look for the boulder with painted arrow for Tiscali and follow it to the left (east) up a very steep mule trail until you arrive finally at a wide ledge with superb views over the Valle Lanaittu. After another 20 to 25 minutes on foot, keep left on the steepest, overhanging part of the mountain and take the narrow path to the right over the rocks to the huge *dolina* (cavern) and entrance to Tiscali. In the half-light of the cavern, the deserted village is a spooky but very moving sight.

**Monte Tiscali is a dramatic setting for the remains of Tiscali Villaggio Nuragico**

### TAKING A BREAK

Have a drink or lunch on the terrace at the **Ristorante Albergo Sant'Elene** (➤ 96).

➕ 165 D3  🕐 May–Sep daily 9–7; Oct–Apr 9–5  💶 Moderate  ❓ Excursions depart from Dorgali. Coop Ghivine (Via Montebello 5, Dorgali; tel: 0784 96721; www.ghivine.com) has departures at 9am, returning at about 4:30. Price €40, including entrance to Tiscali

**Tourist Information**
🎯 Via Deledda, Oliena  🕐 Jun–Aug Mon–Sat 9–1, 4–7, Sun 9–1

**Sa Sedda 'e Sos Carros**
🎯 9:30–6:30  💶 Moderate

## TISCALI VILLAGGIO NURAGICO: INSIDE INFO

**Top tips** It is vital to wear sturdy footwear with a secure grip and ankle support. This is not a trek to take casually.

■ If you don't take a guide, make sure that you advise someone of your movements and your estimated return time.

■ A hat and sunscreen plus an ample supply of water (at least one litre per person) are essential.

# ❸ Golfo di Orosei

Stretching for 40km (25 miles), the Gulf of Orosei has the longest undeveloped coastline in the Mediterranean. Limestone cliffs and rock formations scatter the coastline punctuated by beautiful coves, secluded grottoes and the most glorious hidden beaches.

The gulf is a symmetrical arch extending from Capo Nero in the north to Capo Monte Santo in the south. It is the seafront of the **Supramonte**, a wild and steep coast where holm oak forests, centuries-old juniper trees and *macchia* extend down to the sea. The royal eagle, Eleonora's falcon and griffon vulture are regular residents and these birds of prey can often be seen peeping out from their eyries on the cliff tops.

**Opposite: Grotta del Bue Marino**

**Below: A boat trip along Golfo de Orosei**

### Orosei Town

Much of the architecture in Orosei town is Spanish, reflecting its former rule by the Aragonese. It's a pleasant place to stroll around, starting at the **Piazza del Popolo**, where you'll find the 13th-century **Cattedrale di San Giácomo** with its 18th-century neoclassical facade and gilded interior. On the west side of town the 15th-century **Sant'Antonio Abate** with its Pisan watchtower is worth a look, although it has been extensively restored.

On the coast, Marina di Orosei has a 6km (3.5-mile) quiet stretch of golden sand, framed by pines and lapped by emerald water.

### Grotta del Bue Marino

South down the coast, **Cala Gonone** has a gorgeous setting around a harbour framed by soaring mountains. Once a little fishing village, it took off as a tourist resort when the Grotta del Bue Marino opened in the 1950s.

This is the largest and most dramatically beautiful of the many grottoes on this coast. The *bue marino* ("sea ox") is the local name for the monk seal, common a century ago but now one of the world's most endangered mammals. This cave was one of its last hiding places in Sardinia, although the last sightings were back in 1992. A tour takes you to where fresh and saltwater mingle in lakes and the light playing on the water reveals fantastical pink and white formations in the stalactites

and stalagmites. A relief on the rocky wall at the entrance, showing a dozen dancing figures around a solar disc, has been verified as graffiti from the neolithic period.

## Glorious Beaches

Cala Gonone itself has three wonderful beaches, all within walking distance from the harbour. Other beaches, such as Cala Fuili, Cala Cartoe and beautiful **Cala Luna**, locations in Madonna's movie *Swept Away*, are all within a few kilometres. Accessible only by boat, the coves are surrounded by crystal waters, perfect for swimming and snorkelling. Boat excursions can be arranged on the harbour, or you can catch a shuttle ferry to the sandy beach of Cala Luna.

### TAKING A BREAK

Have lunch at Cala Gonone's **Hotel Pop** (➤ 95).

---

🞥 165 E3

### Grotta del Bue Marino
☎ 078 496243 🕔 Weather permitting, visits Aug daily 9, 10, 11, 12, 3, 4 and 5; Jul 9, 10, 11, 12 and 3; Easter–Jun, Sep, Oct 11 and 3 💶 Expensive

---

### GOLFO DI OROSEI: INSIDE INFO

**Top tip** It is possible to reach **Cala Luna on foot** from the road at Cala Fuili – by a fairly precipitous rough track for around 4km (2.5 miles). The last descent is very stony and something of a scramble. You can always return on one of the **regular boats** back to Cala Gonone port.

# At Your Leisure

### 4 Belvedere on Monte Ortobene

East of Núoro, 8km (5 miles) out of town, the road winds up to Monte Ortobene and its glorious vistas over the valley floor and Supramonte massif. A dusty track leads to 49 steps that climb up to an enormous bronze statue of *Il Redentore (Christ the Redeemer)* at 955m (3,130 feet). The statue shows Christ trampling the devil underfoot and is a site of great pilgrimage. The Sagra del Redentore (► 40), Núoro's most important festival, takes place every year in late August, culminating on 29 August, when a long procession is made here from the cathedral.

This is a very popular spot for a picnic in the surrounding woods, and there are a couple of bars and restaurants as well as stalls selling cold drinks and souvenirs.

➕ 164 C4 🚍 No 8 from Piazza Vittorio Emanuele in Núoro

### 5 Oliena

Only a few kilometres south of Núoro, this mountain town is known for the architecture of its houses, with balconies and leafy courtyards, which you can look into from the stone-paved streets.

Although not as "painted" as Orgosolo, Oliena has several striking wall murals, and in the parish church, Chiesa Santa Maria, is a remarkable Christmas nativity scene with ceramic figures created by a local artist. A market fills the streets on Saturdays from 7am until 2pm.

➕ 164 C4

### 6 Grotta di Ispinigoli

Towering up to 38m (125 feet), the central stalagmite of this cave is the tallest in Europe. From the entrance 280 steps lead 60m (200 feet) into the grotto. Nine streams flow through these extraterrestrial surroundings where the temperature remains at a constant 16–17°C (60–62°F).

Estimated to be 180 million years old, but only discovered in 1927, the grotto has yielded some remarkable finds – including otter fossils dating back to the ice age, bronze and silver bracelets and necklaces. All these items were typically found in Punic burial tombs. Human skeletal remains have also fuelled speculation that this was once a place of human sacrifice.

The Abisso delle Vergini (Abyss of the Virgins) is the well that leads into this second cavity, 40m (130 feet) below. Theories abound such as the possibility that richly bejewelled young women were sacrificed by throwing them down the well. Guides will tell you that it's more probable that it was used as an ancient burial ground. But one thing is certain – the subterranean scene is imbued with an eerie, almost sacred, atmosphere.

➕ 165 E4 ✉ Just off the Orosei–Dorgali road ☎ 078 496 2431 🕐 Mar–Nov daily 9–5; Aug 9–6. Tours depart on the hour lasting 45 minutes 💰 Expensive

**The central stalagmite at Grotta di Ispinigoli is the tallest is Europe**

## 7 Mamoiada

Lying 14km (9 miles) south of Núoro is the town of Mamoiada. Every year at carnival time (➤ 40) this usually colourless town erupts into a frenzy of shaggy-sheepskinned men wearing demonic black wooden masks and weighed down by heavy cowbells. These traditional costumed figures, known as *mamuthones*, have pagan origins, and this ritual is an attempt to drive out demons before the spring. They shuffle along, rattling cowbells behind their backs; they represent defeated men and animals and are subjugated by the *issokadores* – men dressed in red and white wielding lassos. This scene is also re-enacted on 17 January for the Festa di Sant'Antonio. According to legend Sant'Antonio took hell's fire to give to man, and for this festival bonfires are lit throughout the village.

The Museo delle Maschere Mediterranee (Tue–Sun 9–1, 3–7) contains examples of these costumes and others from the Mediterranean basin. These demonstrate the similarities and commonality among the masks and carnival celebrations of various cultures in the region, including the Alps, Spain and the Balkans. This is considered one of the best mask museums in Europe, and its multimedia presentations recreate the experience for those who cannot be there during the winter festival.
➕ 164 C3

## 8 Orgosolo

A painted rock depicting "the greedy landowner of Orgosolo" greets you outside the entrance to this town of murals. More than 150 of them adorn the streets and corners in a tradition dating from 1975. Professor Francesco del Casino and his students decided to celebrate the 30th anniversary of Liberation and the Resistance with political and satirical portrayals. Nowadays, many are devoted to modern-day as well as political themes – from folkloric figures, such as the *mamuthones,* to the destruction of New York's Trade Center on 11 September 2001.

**Walking through Gola Su Gorruppu**

There are, too, allusions to the sheep rustling and kidnappings for which this town was once notorious. Popularly known as the "capital" of the Barbágia, the region's most notorious bandits are said to have taken refuge here in the first half of the 20th century, when the town averaged a murder every two months.

The Festa dell'Assunta takes place in Orgosolo on 15 August – a highlight of Barbágia and one of the top processions of the region.
➕ 164 C3

## 9 Gola Su Gorruppu

This is one of Europe's most spectacular gorges, carved out of limestone by the river Flumineddu, with cliffs soaring to more than 400m (1,300 feet). The colour of the limestone and microclimate within make this an unforgettable experience. The entire length of the gorge is some 8km (5 miles) but you need proper equipment and a guide to venture a long way inside.

By car from Dorgali, take the bypass to the west (SS125) then follow the signpost for the Sant' Elene Hotel. Past the hotel you will pick up signs for Tiscali and, after about 4km (2.5 miles) of unsurfaced road take the left turn signposted Gorruppu and a car park. It is about a two-hour trek to the gorge from here.

✚ 165 D3

**Cooperativa Gorropu**
✉ Via Sa Preda Lada 2, Urzulei
☎ 0782 649282; www.gorropu.com

### ⑩ Monti del Gennargentu

Meaning "silver gate", the Gennargentu is the highest massif in Sardinia and in winter is covered in snow. The Parco del Gennargentu and Parco del Golfo di Orosei have wild mountain terrain and coast covering 73,935ha (182,620 acres). There are many villages dotted around; none are especially attractive, but they make good walking bases. Sardinia's highest village is Fonni, lying at 1,000m (3,280 feet) above sea level. The highest peaks are all accessible from here: Bruncu Spina at 1,829m (6,000 feet) and Punta La Marmora at 1,834m (6,016 feet). The strenuous climb to the top of Punta La Marmora is rewarded with fabulous views over the entire island. For a less demanding foray, it's possible to drive most of the way up to Bruncu Spina to the S'Arena *rifugio* (mountain refuge) at 1,500m (4,920 feet), from where it's a relatively easy hike to the top.

The area is thickly vegetated with holm oak woods surrounded by Mediterranean *macchia*. The lower flanks are cloaked in vineyards that produce the famous red wine made from the Cannonau grape, and this area is also especially noted for its pecorino cheese. Along the coastal cliffs, olive trees, carob trees and juniper thrive in the particularly warm climate.

✚ 164 82

**Museo delle Maschere Mediterranee**
✉ Piazza Europa 15 ☎ 0784 569018; www.museodellemaschere.it ⓒ Tue–Sun 9–1, 3–7 ✋ Moderate

The holm-oak wooded hills of the Gennargentu are surrounded by *macchia*

# Where to...
## Stay

**Prices**

Expect to pay per double room, per night:

€ under €90    €€ €90–€155    €€€ €155–€250    €€€€ over €250

## GOLFO DI OROSEI

### Hotel Su Barchile €€

This very welcoming three-star hotel has 10 rooms housed in a former dairy. It is modern and very comfortable and all rooms are air-conditioned. It also has a highly regarded restaurant (▶ 96).

➕ 165 E4 ⌗ Via Mannu 5, Orosei
☎ 078 498879; www.subarchile.it

### Hotel Costa Dorada €€–€€€

Set between the mountains and sea, this small, family-run hotel is a little jewel set among flower-filled gardens. There are 23 comfortable rooms decorated in traditional Sardinian style and a vine-shaded dining terrace with views over the Gulf of Orosei. The beach is across a small road from the hotel and there are many excursions. In season, it has exclusive use of *The Marlin* – a 55-foot boat (extra cost) to reach hidden coves and beaches.

➕ 165 E4 ⌗ Lungomare Palmasera 45, Cala Gonone ☎ 078 493332; www.hotelcostadorada.it ⊙ Apr–Oct

### Hotel Pop €–€€

Just opposite the port, this friendly three-star hotel is a meeting point for locals. Run by the charismatic Anglophile Simone Spanu and his family, service is excellent, rooms are modern and clean and every kind of excursion can be arranged. There is a lovely terrace outside overlooking the boats. It also has one of the resort's best restaurants, Al Porto (▶ 96).

➕ 165 E4 ⌗ Piazza del Porto 2, Cala Gonone ☎ 078 493185 (348 629 7177 in English); www.hotelpop.it

### Hotel Il Querceto €

On the southwestern side of the town, this three-star property is in the typical mountain style. Rooms are airy and all overlook woodland from their balconies. The attractive gardens also have tennis courts.

➕ 165 D4 ⌗ Via Lamarmora 4, Dorgali ☎ 078 496509; www.ilquerceto.com ⊙ Apr–Oct

## OLIENA

### Hotel Su Gologone €€€

Located 7km (4 miles) northeast of Oliena amid magnificent scenery, perched like a balcony on the Valle di Lanaittu, this is one of Sardinia's loveliest hotels/restaurants. There are 68 rooms and suites, decorated in harmony with the arts and crafts of the region. Most have a balcony. There is a swimming pool, beauty and relaxation centre and 4x4 excursions on offer. The restaurant is also very highly acclaimed (▶ 97).

➕ 164 C4 ⌗ Località Su Gologone ☎ 078 4287512; www.sugologone.it ⊙ Closed Nov to mid-Mar

## MONTE ORTOBENE

### Fratelli Sacchi €–€€

Near the top of Monte Ortobene, this is a good base for immersing yourself in views of the countryside. There are 22 comfortable, clean rooms that are rustic and a little old-fashioned; some have balconies. The restaurant specializes in local Nuorese cuisine and pizzas.

➕ 164 C4 ⌗ Monte Ortobene ☎ 078 431200 ⊙ Apr–Oct

# Where to...
## Eat and Drink

**Prices**

Expect to pay per person for a meal, excluding drinks, tax and tip:

€ under €26    €€ €26–€55    €€€ over €55

### Bar Majore €

Something of an institution, this is Núoro's oldest café. The opulent interior has a frescoed ceiling, gilded stucco and antiques. It's a great place for immersing yourself in the local atmosphere.

🚹 164 C4 ⊠ Corso Garibaldi 71 🕲 Daily lunch and dinner

### Il Rifugio €–€€

Close to Madonna delle Grazie, this bustling trattoria/pizzeria is very popular with the locals. Home-made pasta and pizza are specialities and the pizza makers (pizzaioli) are an entertainment in themselves. The restaurant belongs to the Slow Food movement.

🚹 164 C4 ⊠ Via Antonio Mereu 28/36 🕾 078 423 2355 🕲 Thu–Tue lunch and dinner

### Ristorante Grillo €–€€

The chef at this popular, award-winning in-town restaurant values fresh local vegetables, featuring them in original seasonal dishes. Don't miss the pasta, which is made on the premises.

🚹 164 C4 ⊠ Via Monsignor Melas 1 🕾 078 438668 🕲 Daily lunch and dinner

### Ristorante Albergo Sant'Elene €€

Lying 3km (1.5 miles) off the SS125 from Dorgali, this restaurant is perched on a hillside. From the terrace there are glorious views, and the typical regional cuisine is no less splendid. Roast suckling pig, lamb, grilled fish and appetizers of home-made paté are complemented by good wine and friendly service. There are also excellent pizzas.

🚹 165 D4 ⊠ Località Sant'Elene, Dorgali 🕾 078 494572; www.hotelsantelene.it 🕲 Summer daily; winter Tue–Sun; closed Jan

### Ristorante Al Porto €€

Feast on local delicacies in the locals' favourite restaurant overlooking the port. Host Simone Spanu, affectionately known as Pop, is infectious in his enthusiasm for seafood – fishermen call him as they approach the dock to advise him of the catch of the day. Swordfish, octopus, succulent king prawns and puppy-sized lobsters all feature regularly, along with "Sardinian caviar" (bottarga), here served to perfection with spaghetti. There are also meat dishes.

🚹 165 E4 ⊠ Hotel Pop, Piazza del Porto 2, Cala Gonone 🕾 078 493185 (348 629 7177 in English); www.hotelpop.it 🕲 Daily lunch and dinner

### Su Barchile €€

This very good restaurant prides itself on the traditions of the sea and land combined in natural flavours. Carnivores are well catered for in dishes such as pork with myrtle, but the emphasis is on fish and seafood, with more than 44 dishes on the menu covering everything from spaghetti with lobster to grilled, fresh fish. Try the delicious puddings served with the establishment's own moscato (muscat). The outdoor terrace is perfect for summer dining.

🚹 165 E4 ⊠ Via Mannu 5, Orosei 🕾 078 498879; www.subarchile.it 🕲 Daily lunch and dinner

## Colibrì €€

This warm, welcoming, family-run restaurant specializes in traditional Sardinian cuisine such as *cinghiale* (wild boar) and *porceddu* (suckling pig). It also has good fish dishes.

➕ 165 D4 ☒ Via Gramsci 14 (corner of Via Floris), Dorgali ☎ 078 496054 ⓧ Jul–Aug daily lunch and dinner; Sep–Jun Mon–Sat lunch and dinner

## Costa Dorada €€

The vine-shaded terrace restaurant of this pretty, family-run hotel overlooks the Gulf of Orosei. On offer are fresh catch of the day fish specials as well as meat, all inspired by traditional Sard recipes.

➕ 165 E4 ☒ Lungomare Palmasera 45, Cala Gonone ☎ 078 449 3332 ⓧ Apr–Oct lunch and dinner

## Da Filippo Pizzeria €

More than 100 different types of pizza toppings are on offer at this popular pizzeria. The Oroseina has aubergine purée, and other offerings include the Gennargentu,

with local pecorino cheese and mushrooms, and the Nuragica, with ricotta and honey. At lunchtime there is also a *menu del giorno* (daily menu) with *antipasti di terra e mare* (meat, cheese and seafood). Children's menus are available.

➕ 165 E4 ☒ Via Nazionale 195, Orosei ☎ 078 499 8159; www.pizzeriadafilippo.it ⓧ Daily lunch and dinner

## OLIENA

## Ristorante Masiloghi €€

Located a little way out of town to the east, this is a very good rustic restaurant, with tables spilling out onto a veranda. Specials include *maccarrones a bocciu* (handmade Sardinian gnocchi) and *malloreddus* (ravioli stuffed with sheep cheese or ricotta), spit-roasted or barbecued pork, kid, lamb and wild boar seasoned with aromatic herbs. There is a good wine list. Gourmet tasting menus are also available.

➕ 164 C4 ☒ Via Galiani 68, Oliena ☎ 078 428 5696; www.masiloghi.it ⓧ Daily lunch and dinner

## Su Gologone €€€

This popular restaurant serves Sardinian cuisine based on recipes handed down through generations. Delicious antipasti and home-made pasta, as well as the speciality *porceddu* (suckling pig), feature. There is a vast wine cellar and Oliena fine wines are, as always, a treat. In summer, dine on the outdoor terrace admiring the views.

➕ 164 C4 ☒ Hotel Su Gologone, Località Su Gologone ☎ 078 428 7512; www.sugologone.it ⓧ Daily lunch and dinner

## GROTTA DI ISPINIGOLI

## Hotel/Restaurant Ispinigoli €–€€

Below the grotto entrance, the panoramic restaurant terrace is a good place to relax while waiting for a tour of the grotto. All tastes are catered for, with set menus for vegetarians, seafood, meat options

and special dishes for children as well as an à la carte menu.

➕ 165 E4 ☒ Grotta di Ispinigoli ☎ 078 495266; www.hotelispinigoli.com ⓧ Daily lunch and dinner

## ORGOSOLO

## Bar Podda €

This is a locals' hang out but prices are very reasonable and it's as good a place as any to get the flavour of Orgosolo. Usefully, it is also an internet bar.

➕ 164 C3 ☒ Via Nuoro 7 ☎ 078 440 2165 ⓧ Daily lunch and dinner

## Restaurant/Hotel Ai Monti del Gennargentu €€

Around 5km (3 miles) from Orgosolo, this pleasant restaurant with rooms, set among oak trees, is well placed for discovering the local mountain sights. The restaurant specializes in traditional mountain food, based on Sardinian meats.

➕ 164 C3 ☒ Località Settiles ☎ 078 440 2374 ⓧ Daily lunch and dinner

# Where to... Shop

## NÚORO

In Núoro there is an **ISOLA** outlet (▶ 39) for authentic handmade crafts at Corso Garibaldi 58 (tel: 078 433581; Mon–Sat 9–1, 4–8). For gourmet delicacies visit **Tavola degli Antichi** at Via Trieste 70 (tel: 078 435501). Specialities include *aranzada di Núoro* (candied orange peel and honey), and almond biscuits known as *saranzata*.

## DORGALI

In Dorgali you will find **Esca Dolciaria** (Viale Kennedy, tel: 078 494472; wwwescadolciaria.it), an excellent shop specializing in pastries, typical of the Dorgali region and traditional confections.

# Where to... Be Entertained

## ACTIVITIES

The area around Núoro is very scenic, hilly and untamed. The environment is host to many species of birds, from game to birds of prey. Following the old shepherds' trails, you walk in the tracks of wild boar, weasels, martens and foxes. The mountains around Oliena are full of grottoes and passageways where there are superb opportunities for climbing and canyoning. Two co-operatives offer hikes, walks, rock climbing and cave- and canyon-exploration trips in the Gulf of Orosei and Gennargentu region: **Cooperativa Ghivine** (Via Lamarmora 69e, Dorgali; tel: 078 49672 1; www.ghivine.com/excursions.htm)

and **Cooperativa Gorropu** (Via Sa Preda Lada 2, Urzulei; tel: 078 264 9282; www.gorropu.com).

For excursions including trekking, cross-country driving, canyoning, mountain-biking, caving, archaeology and diving, contact **Consortium Atlantikà** (Via Lamarmora 195, Dorgali, tel: 328 972 9719; www.atlantika.it). For quad biking, contact **Barbágia Insolita** (Corso Vittorio Emanuele 48, Oliena, tel: 078 428 6005; www.barbagiainsolita.it).

If you want to explore the coast alone, rent a **motorboat** in Cala Gonone from one of the companies with kiosks on the harbour front. Cala Gonone is also a good centre for **diving** and there are several clubs such as the Argonauta, Via dei Lecci 10 (tel: 078 493046;

www.argonauta.it). On offer are guided snorkelling tours accompanied by professional guides; dives on World War II wrecks, caverns, and shallow dives and all levels of PADI dive courses. Special activities also include night diving.

## NIGHTLIFE

Nightlife is fairly limited in this part of the island. There are a few bars in Núoro and one club, the **Boca Chica**, at Via Mughina 94 (tel: 329 312 0010) which has a Mexican theme and plays Latino-style music. Cala Gonone becomes very lively in summer, with several discos alongside the Spiaggia Palmasera on the southern end. There are several bars, too, such as the **Roadhouse Blues** (Lungomare Palmasera) on the seafront and the popular cocktail bar at the **Hotel Bue Marino** (Via Vespucci 8, ▶ 96). Monte Ortobene has a couple of bars that hold events in summer.

# Sássari and the Northwest

# Getting Your Bearings

The northwest has a different character from the rest of the island. It also has pretty seaside resorts, long beaches, fine churches, nature reserves, countryside littered with *nuraghi*, Sardinia's second city and a very picturesque seaside Catalan city. But it is generally less rural and, in places, is more reminiscent of the Italian mainland and of Spain.

The northern corner has the Parco Nazionale dell'Asinara, a nature reserve that is home to rare miniature albino donkeys and ringed by glorious white beaches that meld into turquoise waters. The jumping-off point for the island is the little seaside resort of Stintino, with the nearby Spiaggia della Pelosa – formerly one of the island's most beautiful beaches but diminished by recent sea erosion. Nearby Porto Tórres is a blot on the landscape with its petrochemical works and oil refinery and few vestiges of its former glory as the principal Roman port. However, the main Carlo Felice highway conveniently links this salty port to the rest of the island and to Stintino, where the handsome Pisan Basilica di San Gavino, Sardinia's largest Romanesque church, is worth investigating.

**Below: The marina in Alghero**

Inland Sássari is a vibrant university town with a lovely old medieval quarter and is second only to the capital, Cágliari. Alghero, too, has a tangle of medieval alleys and sits at the head of the Riviera del Corallo (Coral Riviera). From the harbour near its beautiful beaches there's easy access by boat to Neptune's Grotto (Grotta di Nettuno), one of Sardinia's top sights.

The scenic coastal drive south to the pretty riverside town of Bosa is sprinkled with beaches off the road, while inland lies "The Way of the Churches", the Valle dei Nuraghi and Nuraghe Santu Antíne, one of Sardinia's biggest and best *nuraghi*.

## ★ Don't Miss

## At Your Leisure

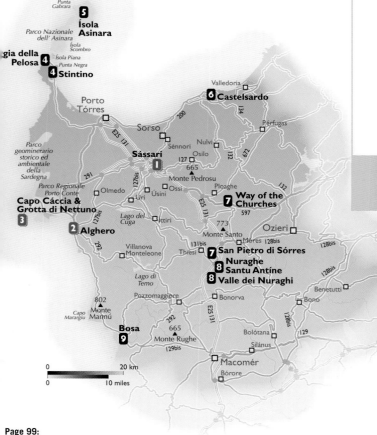

**Page 99:**
**Santissima**
**Trinità di**
**Saccargia,**
**Sássari province**

# In Three Days

If you're not quite sure where to begin your travels, this itinerary recommends a practical and enjoyable three days exploring Sássari and the northwest of the island, taking in some of the best places to see using the Getting Your Bearings map on the previous page. For more information see the main entries.

## Day 1

### Morning
Travel to – or wake up in – **❶ Sássari** (➤ 104–105). Visit the compact old town and, at its heart, the baroque Duomo on its eponymous piazza. A short walk southwards to Piazza Santa Maria brings you to Santa Maria di Betlem and the massive wooden candles, *candelieri*. Have coffee at Florian (➤ 114) on Via Roma. Cross the Piazza Italia (above) into Corso Vittorio Emanuele II. Browse around shops and marvel at the Teatro Cívico.

### Lunch
Have lunch at the Liberty Restaurant/Piano Bar (➤ 114).

### Afternoon
From Sássari drive the 36km (22 miles) to **❷ Alghero** (➤ 106–107, top right) and head for the beach – Spiaggia Le Bombarde, west of Fertilia, is the best. Walk around the *centro storico* (historic centre) and visit the excellent tourist office. Have a drink at Café Latino (➤ 114–115) overlooking the port. Enjoy the shops and evening *passeggiata*, then have dinner at Angedras Restaurant, with views over the harbour (➤ 114).

# Day 2

### Morning

Drive from Alghero along the Riviera del Corallo past the curious town of Fertilia, laid out in rigid grid-system by Mussolini, past the lovely Porto Conte bay to Capo Cáccia. Visit the **3 Grotta di Nettuno** (➤ 108). Have a welcome mid-morning cappuccino at the bar at the top of the steps. Drive northwest on the superstrada SS131

Carlo Felice highway bypassing Porto Tórres to **4 Stintino** (➤ 110), stopping at one of the beaches south of the town.

### Lunch

Have lunch in Stintino at Bar Skipper di Lagorio (Lungomare Colombo 57, tel 079 523460) or at any of the beach bars.

### Afternoon

Drive east to **6 Castelsardo** (➤ 110–111) arriving in time to see it bathed in rosy late afternoon sunlight. Stroll through the tangle of little lanes leading up to the Castello, and stay the night. (Alternatively, spend the night in Stintino and take the full-day excursion to **5 Ísola Asinara** (➤ 110, below) the following morning.)

# Day 3

### Morning

Drive south to San Pietro de Sórres (➤ 111) and nearby **8 Nuraghe Santu Antíne** (➤ 111–112). Have coffee at the bar at the entrance to the *nuraghe* site. Drive west to Bosa.

### Lunch

Several cafés and restaurants overlook the beach in Bosa Marina.

### Afternoon

Take the scenic coast road from **9 Bosa to Alghero** (➤ 112), stopping off to admire the views and visiting the little beaches. Stay overnight in Alghero.

# ❶ Sássari

After Cágliari, this is Sardinia's second city – although the Sassarese will tell you that it is the first. It is sophisticated, cheerful, has a thriving café scene and a fascinating *centro storico*, or historical centre. National politicians, including Antonio Segni, Francesco Cossiga and Enrico Berlinguer, have been nurtured here in this, Sardinia's oldest university town.

## The Medieval Town

At the core of the *centro storico*, the 15th-century **Duomo di San Nicola** has a baroque fantasy facade, added in the 18th century and very reminiscent of Puglian baroque you can see in Lecce in the south of Italy. The interior is by comparison very bare, although it does contain some works of art, such as the *Madonna con Bambino* by a 16th-century Sardinian artist, which adorns the high altar, and walnut choirstalls.

Around here the lively narrow streets of the old medieval town are perfect for a stroll. Inevitably you will end up at the **Corso Vittorio Emanuele II**. This street is full of *palazzi*, gorgeous wrought-iron balconies and handsome buildings – all in different states of neglect or,

**The elaborate facade of Duomo di San Nicola**

more recently, restoration. The lovely Liberty-style **Teatro Cívico** has been beautifully restored and its jewel-box interior is like a miniature version of Milan's La Scala.

North of here, along Corso Trinità, are remnants of the city's **medieval walls**, while the nearby **Fontana di Rosello** is a splendid Renaissance fountain sculpted in marble and dark stone. At each side there are statues of the four seasons with four white dolphin mouth spouts and eight lion-head spouts.

At Piazza di Santa Maria, close to the site of the original city walls, is the **Chiesa di Santa Maria di Betlem**. Founded in 1106, it has a lovely Romanesque facade, while the inside is more overblown baroque. The lateral chapels display the *candelieri* (giant wooden candles) that represent the town's medieval craft guilds and are paraded for the big 14 August festival, I Candelieri (➤ 13, 40). Made from wood and polychrome, they are around 420cm (160 inches) in height and weigh 310kg (685lb).

### Around Piazza Italia

All roads lead to the heart of town on the **Piazza Italia**. But a stroll along the **Via Roma** just off the piazza is always a delight, as this is the centre of Sássari's thriving café life.

### TAKING A BREAK

Enjoy a drink at **Florian** (► 114), just off Piazza Italia.

Below: Palazzo della Provincia on Piazza Italia, Sássari's grandest square

➕ 158 C4

**Duomo di San Nicola**
✉ Piazza Duomo 🕐 Daily 9–12, 4–7 💲 Free

**Chiesa di Santa Maria di Betlem**
✉ Piazza di Santa Maria 🕐 Daily 7:15–12, 5–8

---

## SÁSSARI: INSIDE INFO

**In more depth** Up to 12 men carry one *candeliero* in the **I Candelieri festival** (► 13, 40). Local dignitaries watch from the balcony of Teatro Cívico; they clap if they like the decoration of the giant candlesticks and boo if they don't.

**One to miss** Near the Duomo is, arguably, the ugliest square in Sardinia, Piazza Mazzotti, once a notorious red-light area that was demolished to create a soulless space; its saving grace is the very good Pizzeria da Bruno (► 114).

# 2 Alghero

The picturesque medieval city is beautifully positioned amid white beaches, on Sardinia's "Riviera del Corallo" – a reference to the famed local red coral. Bathed in a warm pink glow, it sits on a small peninsula surrounded by towers and fortifications. In this tourist town and fishing port the lovely old centre has a tangle of narrow lanes filled with bars, restaurants and shops. It also has a distinct Catalan character as a result of Spanish colonization in the 14th century.

### Exploring the Old Town

The best place to start is at the excellent tourist information centre (➤ 33) in Piazza Porta Terra, the old main entrance to the city. Near by is the **Torre di Porta Terra**, a multimedia museum and panoramic terrace from where there are views of the town and majolica dome of the **Chiesa di San Michele**.

The stone streets of the old city, narrow and lined with shops displaying coral jewellery, are often bridged by arches, and are dotted randomly by small *piazze* (squares). The "main" street of the old town is narrow Via Carlo Alberto.

**San Michele** dominates the skyline with its glistening ceramic dome and is perhaps the most opulent of the Jesuits' baroque churches on the island. The interior is full of sumptuous stucco and fine altar paintings. **San Francesco**, with its stately, pointed Aragonese tower, hosts summer evening concerts.

Alghero's **Cattedrale** interior is a mixture of architectural styles, but the impressive dome dates from the 18th century.

*Bastioni (walls) encircle the waterfront*

## The Waterfront

The waterfront is girded by the *bastoni* (walls), and a walk along here makes a perfect evening *passeggiata*. The beaches in the immediate area have fine, white sand, but seaweed can sometimes be a problem: Alghero derives its name from the abundance of seaweed (*alghe*) in the surrounding waters. The best beaches are north of the town and the Lido on the way to Fertilia.

### TAKING A BREAK

Have an *aperitivo* or lunchtime snack at **Il Ghiotto (di Roberto Peana)** in Piazza Civica (➤ 114).

Parts of the cloister in Chiesa di San Francesco date back to the 13th century

➕ 158 B3

**Torre di Porta Terra**

➕ 170 C2  ✉ Piazza Porta Terra  ☎ 079 973 4045  🕐 Summer daily 9–1, 5–9  💷 Inexpensive  ❓ Display panels are in Italian only

**Chiesa di San Michele**

➕ 170 B1  ✉ Via Carlo Alberto  🕐 Daily from 20 minutes before Mass

**Chiesa di San Francesco**

➕ 170 B2  ✉ Via Carlo Alberto  🕐 Mon–Sat 9:30–12, 5–7:30, Sun 5–7:30

**Cattedrale**

➕ 170 B2  ✉ Piazza Duomo  🕐 Daily 7–12, 5–7:30. Campanile Tue, Thu, Sat 7–9:30pm; at other times tel: 079 973 3041

---

## ALGHERO: INSIDE INFO

**Top tips** North of Alghero, near the airport, **Necropoli di Anghelu Ruju** is one of Sardinia's most important ancient sites with 38 tombs carved into the sandstone between 3000BC and 1500BC. You can enter some interiors to see carvings above the low doorways (tel: 079 989 7502; Nov–Feb daily 10–2; Mar daily 9:30–4; Apr–Oct 9–7).

■ Opposite the Necropoli, **Sella and Mosca Vineyard** (➤ 116) produces some of the island's top-quality wines. There are free guided tours daily plus a shop (tel: 079 997700; Jun to mid-Oct).

# 3 Capo Cáccia and Grotta di Nettuno

One of the top sights on the island is just to the west of Alghero. The limestone rock of the Capo Cáccia promontory has been buffeted and sculpted by wave and wind for 135 million years. From the lookout point there are glorious views over the cape and Ísola Foradada, while around the headland is the spectacular, giddying Escala del Cabirol (literally "goat's steps" in Catalan). This 654-step descent leads to the famous Grotta di Nettuno.

The stunning deep cavern with a lake is known as **Neptune's Grotto**, the mythical abode of nymphs. It is filled with **stalactites and stalagmites** twisted into fantastical shapes – a subterranean fairyland populated by shapes resembling human beings, statues, trees and animals. All is bathed in colour ranging from greenish-blue to white, yellow and orange crystals from the shimmering phosphorescence of the rock.

**A tour** of the Grotto takes you 200m (220 yards) around the shores of a saltwater lake, Lamarmora, facing the Acquasantiera – or holy water font – a huge 2m-high (6.5-foot) stalagmite. As the natural light ends and the darkness begins, shapes such as the Great Organ eerily seem to come to life. Guides fondly remember when visitors could row across the lake, lit by thousands of small candles on little plates floated on the water, creating an otherworldly glow of enchantment in the grand chamber. Let your imagination run free with the enchanting spectacle of those tiny, quivering flames throwing shadows on the wall and the reflections in the still waters of the lake.

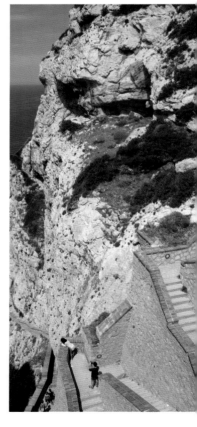

**Above: Grotta di Nettuno with its limestone formations**

**Left: Steps down to the cave cling to the sheer cliff face**

## Getting There

There are two ways to reach the grotto from Alghero. By sea, **a boat trip** from the town port takes about an hour to get there. You pass by the Cape Galera and Punto Giglio cliffs, then round the tip of Capo Cáccia to arrive at the mouth of the caves lying at the foot of a towering cliff – a hugely impressive sight.

Overland by car, the caves are 24km (15 miles) from Alghero. The **panoramic road** (SS127) curves around Capo Cáccia, unfurling one of Sardinia's best views, taking in the bay of Porto Conte, Alghero itself, and stretching as far south as the Bosa coastline. There is a car park at Capo Cáccia.

### TAKE A BREAK

At the top of the steps leading down to the Grotta di Nettuno there is a **bar** serving refreshing drinks and ice creams.

🔓 158 A3 ✉ Capo Cáccia ☎ 079 946540 🕐 Guided tours every hour Apr–Sep daily 9–7; Oct 9–5; Jan–Mar, Nov–Dec 9–4 💰 Expensive 🚤 Jun–Sep from Alghero 9:15, 3:10, 5:10; from Capo Cáccia 12, 4:05, 6:05; Oct–May 9:15 and 12 departures only

### CAPO CÁCCIA AND GROTTA DI NETTUNO: INSIDE INFO

**Top tips** Tours of the cave go on the hour – so try to time it so you don't have to hang around. They last 45 minutes and are led single-file by guides.

■ The **Escala del Cabirol** is steep and not suitable for anyone suffering from vertigo. It takes around 15 minutes to make the descent – rather longer on the way back up.

■ **Boats operate** from a tiny marina just before the entrance to the grotto.

■ The waves around Capo Cáccia can become very high, and in rough weather the grotto is closed.

# At Your Leisure

## 4 Stintino and Spiaggia della Pelosa

Boats in the harbour at Stintino

Once among Sardinia's most beautiful sand beaches, Pelosa has been seriously eroded by the sea, although the turquoise waters that wash what's left are as beautiful as ever, and the setting below the formidable black rock hulk of Capo Falcone is still impressive, guarded by a Spanish watchtower.

The pastel buildings of Stintino surround its attractive little harbour, the departure point for boats to Ísola Asinara. South of town are the long white beaches of Spiaggia Saline.

➕ Stintino 158 B5;
Spiaggia della Pelosa 158 A5

## 5 Ísola Asinara

"Donkey Island" became a national park in 1997, but its chequered history includes use as a maximum security penal centre until the 1970s. It takes its name from the island's unique population of miniature albino donkeys, who, along with pigs and mouflons (wild sheep), are its only inhabitants. The sea is cobalt blue and shallow, the white sandy beaches are beautiful – and they are not crowded as access is only possible on authorized excursions from Stintino. Transport is by bus, road train (*trenino*) or four-wheel drive, but you will need to bring your own refreshments.

➕ 158 A2 (inset)

## 6 Castelsardo

The imposing medieval citadel of Castelsardo perches on a rocky outcrop with a jumble of houses at its feet. Known in the 12th century as Castelgenovese, by the mid-15th century it had become Castelaragonese; its strategic importance has long since disappeared but it is still a popular landmark. The main sights are in the Old Town up the steep steps and streets where, apart from the castle, the Cattedrale di Sant'Antonio Abate is worth a look. From the top of the castle there are splendid views – right across to Corsica, on a clear day.

The town is known for its handicrafts, especially *l'intreccio* (straw-weaving) – there's a museum devoted to it in the castle – ceramics, cork and wooden masks.

🚹 159 D5

### Cattedrale di Sant'Antonio Abate
🕓 Summer daily 7am–8pm; winter 7–5:30. Crypt: Mon–Sat 10–1, 3–8

### Castello Museum
☎ 079 471380  🕓 Apr–Oct 9–1, 2–4; Nov–Mar 9:30–1, 3–5:30  🎫 Inexpensive

## ⑦ Way of the Churches and San Pietro de Sórres

The Logudoro (literally "place of gold") south and east of Sássari is lovely, rolling countryside, dotted with Romanesque churches left by the Pisans; the SS597, branching off towards Ólbia, is known as the "Way of the Churches". About 16km (10 miles) southeast of Sássari, the 12th-century Basilica della SS Trinità di Saccargia dominates the countryside – a near-perfect example of Pisan Romanesque style. Dark volcanic basalt contrasts with light limestone stripes and its campanile soars 40m (130 feet) high. Other

**The medieval town of Castelsardo**

churches line the route, then some 16km (10 miles) farther east, perched majestically on a rocky outcrop, you come to Sant' Antíoco di Bisarcio. Dating from the 11th century and combining both Pisan and French influences, it is still grandiose although its campanile – built like a castle keep – has been gravely damaged by lightning.

Farther south, off the SS131, the striped white limestone and black trachyte facade of San Pietro de Sórres, one of Sardinia's best preserved Romanesque churches, overlooks the Valley of the Nuraghi (► below). In its grounds Benedictine monks restore old books and manuscripts in their workshop.

### Basilica della SS Trinità di Saccargia
🚹 159 D3  🕓 Apr–Oct daily 9–dusk
🎫 Inexpensive

### Sant'Antíoco di Bisarcio
🚹 159 E3  🕓 Daily 9–1, 4–7 (but variable)
🎫 Inexpensive

### San Pietro de Sórres
🚹 159 D2  🕓 Daily 9:30–12, 3:30–7:30

## ⑧ Valle dei Nuraghi and Nuraghe Santu Antíne

Torralba is at the head of the Valle dei Nuraghi (Valley of the Nuraghi), 30km (19 miles) south of Sássari. The valley is strewn with ancient complexes, but the biggest is the

Nuraghe Santu Antíne. The central dry-stone tower, made of basalt blocks, towers up to 17m (56 feet) high. It was perhaps up to 21m (69 feet) higher when it was built in around 1500BC, but it was partially demolished in the 19th century to build the village well in Torralba. Three later, smaller towers surround the compound, linked by trenches and corridors. A spiral ramp leads to the central tower's higher rooms. The Romans converted them into a fortress and they were transformed into a palace, known as "Sa Domo de Su Rei", by the early Christians.

Signposted from Santu Antíne, Sant'Andrea Priu is a complex of tombs carved into a rock cliff, dating to between 4000BC and 3000BC. Used into medieval times as chapels, some still show early Christian frescoes. Hours are irregular; call ahead for an appointment (tel: 348 564 2611) or if the gate is closed, upper tombs are still accessible by a path reached from the road beyond.

✚ 159 E2

**Nuraghe Santu Antíne**
✉ About 4km (2.5 miles) south of Torralba
🕐 Apr–Oct daily 9–dusk; Nov–Mar 9–5
💰 Moderate

## 9 Bosa

The SP105 from Alghero to Bosa is a gloriously undulating stretch of 42km (26 miles) of coastal road, skirting little coves and swathes of golden-white sands before arriving at Bosa. This charming town is clustered around the banks of the River Temo, crossed by the Ponte Vecchio bridge. There is a castle standing sentinel over the town, a cathedral and a medieval quarter, Sa Costa, with a fascinating tangle of alleys. The castle chapel, Nostra Signora di Regnos Altos, contains a wonderful 14th-century fresco cycle of famous saints. This ancient town was founded by the Carthaginians and was very prosperous until the 16th century. Its fortunes seem to be on the upward spiral again, and many of the houses have recently been lovingly restored.

Across the Ponte Vecchio and left about 2km (1 mile), the Romanesque San Pietro ex Muras was originally Bosa's cathedral, but was replaced when the village moved nearer to the sea. Notice the reuse of carved stone Roman sarcophagi, a holy water font and architrave over the portal.

✚ 158 C7

**Castello Malaspina and Chiesa di Nostra Signora di Regnos Altos**
☎ 333 544 5675 🕐 Apr–Jun, Sep–Oct daily 10–1, 3:30–6; Jul 10–1, 4–7.30; Aug 10–7:30; Oct–Mar Sat–Sun 10–1, 3:30–6
💰 Inexpensive

**A ruined castle sits above the pretty town of Bosa, which is alongside the River Temo**

# Where to...
## Stay

**Prices**

Expect to pay per double room, per night:

€ under €90    €€ €90–€155    €€€ €155–€250    €€€€ over €250

## SÁSSARI

### Hotel Vittorio Emanuele €–€€

In the heart of the city, this pleasing former *palazzo* has been fully restored. The result is carefully furnished, comfortable rooms where style veers to modern minimalist, but not without murals. All the rooms have air conditioning and are soundproofed. There is a good restaurant, Platha de Cothinas, and a rustic stone cellar – perfect for wine-tasting.

🚩 158 C4 ⊠ Corso Vittorio Emanuele II 100/102 ☎ 079 235538; www.hotelvittorioemanuele.ss.it

## ALGHERO

### Hotel San Francesco €€

A former convent, this is Alghero's only hotel in the old town and a perfect retreat. The best rooms overlook the cloisters of the Chiesa di San Francesco. The included breakfast is taken in the cloisters. There's no parking, but a nearby garage is available for €5 per night.

🚩 170 B2 ⊠ Via Ambrogio Machin 2 ☎ 079 980330; www.sanfrancescohotel.com

### Agriturismo Vessus €

This family-run countryside hotel is an oasis set in olive groves and attractive gardens where the 11 traditional-style rooms, with air conditioning, encircle the swimming pool. The very good restaurant specializes in traditional Sardinian food and includes home-grown fruit, vegetables and, of course, olives and olive oil. The restaurant is open only from June to September for dinner.

🚩 158 B2 ⊠ SS292 per Villanova Monteleone Km 1.85 (3km/2 miles south of Alghero) ☎ 079 973 5018; www.vessus.it

### Hotel Villa Las Tronas €€€–€€€€

Spectacularly located on a private promontory overlooking the sea, this former Italian royal family holiday home is Alghero's most luxurious hotel. Antiques, marbled halls, chandeliers and rich brocades ooze opulence in this 19th-century castellated pleasure palace. There are two saltwater swimming pools, indoor and outdoor, a beauty centre, gym and a wellness centre.

🚩 158 B3 ⊠ Lungomare Valencia 1 ☎ 079 981818; www.hotelvillalastronas.it

## BOSA

### Corte Fiorita €–€€

In three different historic buildings, this collection of *albergi* (inns) is in the heart of town. The rooms are rustic, light and spacious, with tiled floors, exposed stone walls and tasteful fabrics; some have balconies. Breakfast can be taken in a walled courtyard at Le Palme, the check-in point for all properties.

🚩 158 C1 ⊠ Lungo Temo De Gasperi 45 ☎ 078 537 7058; www.albergo-diffuso.it

### Locanda Il Melograno €

Sparkling new guest rooms look straight out at the castle from their hillside perch, in a setting of vines and olive trees. Families will be comfortable here, as the English-speaking owners have small children of their own. No need to go back into town in the evening – the locals come here to dine on fresh produce from valley farms.

🚩 158 C1 ⊠ Località Tiria 1 ☎ 339 469717; www.locandailmelograno.com

# Where to...
# Eat and Drink

## Prices

Expect to pay per person for a meal, excluding drinks, tax and tip:

€ under €26    €€ €26–€55    €€€ over €55

## SÁSSARI

### Ristorante Pizzeria da Bruno €

Enjoy good pizzas and pasta on the outdoor terrace, looking toward the rooftops of the old town and ignoring the graceless square, where 1960s concrete meets medieval town. Unlike most restaurants, it is open Sunday evening.

✚ 158 C4 ⊠ Piazza Mazzotti 12
☎ 079 235573 ⓘ Daily lunch and dinner

### Florian €€

Elegantly mirrored and muralled, both Bar Caffè Florian and the more expensive next-door restaurant are good spots for dining. Tables spill onto the pavement from the bar's Toulouse-Lautrec-inspired interior, perfect for enjoying a *spremuta di arancia* (freshly squeezed blood orange juice) or cappuccino.

✚ 158 C4 ⊠ Bar Caffè Florian, Via Roma 6 ⊠ Florian, Via Capitano Bellieni 27
☎ 079 200 8056 ⓘ Mon–Sat lunch and dinner

### Ristorante Liberty €€

Set in a small piazza in the town centre, next to the Corso Vittorio Emanuele, this elegantly restored restaurant was a small Liberty-style *palazzo*. The speciality is fish. The atmospheric wine/piano bar, with a stream running down the stone steps into the tasting cellar, serves a good selection of snacks.

✚ 158 C4 ⊠ Piazza N Sauro 3
☎ 079 236361 ⓘ Mon–Sat lunch and dinner

### Bar Ristorante Mokador €

This buzzing little place is popular with the locals and a good choice for inexpensive snacks and drinks. On Fridays there is happy hour 7–9pm, with *antipasti all'italiana*.

✚ 158 C4 ⊠ Largo Cavallotti 2, off Piazza Castello, near Via Roma ☎ 079 235736
ⓘ Daily lunch and dinner

## ALGHERO

### Angedras Restaurant €€

Chef Alessandro Tesi prepares a short, well-chosen menu featuring seafood tasting plates (*degustazione di mare*), home-made pasta, such as *spaghetti alla chitarra con vongole e fiori du zucca* (spaghetti with clams and courgette flowers), and meat-based dishes, too. Portions are more nouvelle cuisine than gargantuan in size in this new, minimalist-style restaurant. Outdoor seating overlooks the port and sunset.

✚ 170 A2 ⊠ Via Cavour 31, corner of Bastioni Marco Polo 41 ☎ 079 073 5078;
www.angedrasrestaurant.it ⓘ Daily lunch and dinner

### Il Ghiotto (di Roberto Peana) €

This "snackeria" specializes in *prodotti tipici* – cold cuts of meat and salami, cheeses, pizza, salads and sandwiches. There's a buffet lunch, but you can opt just to have an *aperitivo* and enjoy a free tasting of the various goodies. The attached shop has tempting displays of Sardinian specialities.

✚ 170 B2 ⊠ Piazza Civica 23 ☎ 079 974820 ⓘ Daily lunch buffet 12:30–3:30

### Café Latino €–€€

Overlooking the port, this is the perfect spot to enjoy a drink under the white parasols or inside among the cool stone vaults. Good snacks include panini, pizzas and delicious ice creams.

**🕂 170 B2 ⊠ Bastioni Magellano 10 ☎ 079 976541 ⏰ Jul–Aug daily 9am–11pm; closed Sep–Jun Tue**

### Bella Napoli €–€€

Neapolitan-owned pizzeria with generous portions and good pasta dishes as well as pizzas. Inside it's lively; outside there's a parasol-shaded terrace. Good pasta dishes include ravioli with ricotta cheese and *penne alla Siciliana*.

**🕂 170 B2 ⊠ Piazza Civica 29 ☎ 079 983014 ⏰ Thu–Tue lunch and dinner**

### Trattoria Al Refettorio €€

Chic, atmospheric wine bar with good nibbles to accompany your *aperitivo*. The restaurant food is also good – and there is outdoor, covered seating. Fish and seafood as well as dishes such as wild boar and other carnivorous delights feature. As you would expect, it has a very good, extensive wine list.

**🕂 170 B2 ⊠ Carrerò del Porxo (Vicolo Adami) 47, off Via Roma ☎ 079 973 1126; www.alrefettorio.it ⏰ Wed–Mon lunch and dinner**

### Villa Las Tronas €€–€€€

Reserve a table for sunset – the entire west wall of the elegant hotel (▶ 113) dining room is glass and overlooks the sea. The menu equals the view, a selection of creative dishes based on fresh ingredients, expertly prepared and served by professional staff. Local fish is superbly presented, and the chef shines with meats, whether it's a preparation of lamb rack or a savoury *ragù*. The wine list equals the menu, and is not overpriced.

**🕂 158 B3 ⊠ Lungimare Valencia 1 ☎ 079 981818; www.villalastronas.com ⏰ Daily lunch and dinner**

## STINTINO

### Ristorante da Antonio €€

Set on a road back from the sea, this welcoming family-run restaurant specializes in fish and seafood. The *pane carasau* "music bread" (▶ 23, 38) is excellent and the grilled fresh tuna fish is sublime and goes especially well with the very good rosé Sella and Mosca wine from Alghero. Note that portions tend to be very generous and service is also very attentive.

**🕂 158 B5 ⊠ Via Marco Polo 16 ☎ 079 523077 ⏰ Daily lunch and dinner**

## BOSA

### Borgo Sant'Ignazio €€

Follow the signs through the tangle of alleys of the old town up to this atmospheric bistro, with some tables outside. Specialities include local *aragosta* (lobster) as well as traditional Sardinian meat dishes. As it is on the Strada della Malvasia di Bosa (vineyards), it also has a good selection of Malvasia dessert wines to accompany typical Sardinian sweetmeats.

**🕂 158 C1 ⊠ Via Sant'Ignazio 33 ☎ 078 537 4662 ⏰ Tue–Sun 1–3, 7.30–11**

### Sa Pischedda €€

Under the same ownership as the hotel of this name, this excellent restaurant is part of the Slow Food movement. Prepare to linger over seasonal delicacies and Sardinian specialities and enjoy a glass of Malvasia wine with your pudding. Also run by the hotel is the Ponte Vecchio, on a jetty above the river, which specializes in seafood in a very romantic setting.

**🕂 158 C1 ⊠ Via Roma 8 ☎ 078 537 3065; www.hotelsapischedda.it ⏰ Apr–Sep daily lunch and dinner; Oct–Mar Wed–Mon**

## CASTELSARDO

### La Guardiola €€

With its knockout sunset views over the town and bay, it's easy to forgive the restaurant its fussy presentations and concentrate on the flavours and the setting.

**🕂 159 D5 ⊠ Piazza Bastione 4 ☎ 079 470755; www.ristorantelaguardiola.com ⏰ Jun–Sep daily lunch and dinner; Oct–May Tue–Sun**

# Where to...
## Shop

In **Alghero** shop for clothes, shoes and leather goods, locally crafted ceramics, pottery, cork and hand-woven baskets. There is also a huge choice of jewellery shops, mostly specializing in the unique local red coral. The modern side of town starts at **Via XX Settembre**, where there are larger shops, perfumeries and boutiques. There's a daily fresh fish, fruit and vegetable market in Via Sássari, a large street market on Wednesday morning and a collectors' market on the last Sunday in the month. At **Sella and Mosca Vineyards** (▶ 107), 10km (6 miles) north of Alghero, you can taste and buy their celebrated red wine (www.sellaemosca.com).

**Bosa** is at the centre of vineyards – the Strada della Malvasia di Bosa – and is famous especially for its Malvasia wine. For Sard crafts, such as filigree work, coral, ceramics, traditional knives, embroidery and tablecloths, visit **Deriu** (Artiginiato Sardo e Souvenir) at Via Gioberti 14 (tel: 078 537 5037).

In **Sássari** visit the markets, such as the covered market for fish (closed Mon), plus vegetables and meat. There's also a Sardinian crafts market in front of the Garibaldi statue (closed Mon). **Bagella**, at Corso Vittorio Emanuele 20 (tel: 079 235033; www.bagella.it), one of Sássari's oldest shops, specializes in authentic traditional Sardinian clothing, such as velvet suits, shirts, leather accessories and boots. **Mura** (di Elisabetta e Luisa Branca) at Via Roma 12 (tel: 079 235332) is a chic gift shop with jewellery, silver, decorative objects and antiques.

# Where to...
## Be Entertained

In **Alghero**, the **Teatro Civico** (tel: 079 997800) is in Piazza Vittorio Emanuele in the Old Town. There is live music and bowling at **Poco Loco**, Via Gramsci 8 (tel: 079 973 1034), just off the main seafront promenade, Piazza Sulis. In high summer there are plenty of clubs and discos and the best place (currently) is south of the centre, along the Lungomare, but venues do tend to come and go. Just out of town, the **Ruscello** lies north on the Olmedo road and has open-air dancing and live bands (tel: 339 235 0755; Jul–Aug nightly).

**Sássari** has a thriving cultural scene with several theatres, including the **Teatro Civico** in Corso Vittorio Emanuele (tel: 079 232182) and **Teatro Ferroviario** at Corso Vico 14 (tel: 079 263 3049).

You can get information about what's on from the tourist office. As you would expect from a university town, there are plenty of good, buzzing bars, especially along the Via Roma and in Piazza Castello.

WATERSPORTS

For excursions from Stintino to the Parco Nazionale dell'Asinara including Land Rover drives, contact the **Azienda Mare e Natura**, Via Sássari 77 (tel: 079 520097).

For boat trips from Alghero aboard the sailing boat **Andrea Jensen**, including helping with steering and sail-rigging plus swimming and snorkelling, telephone 333 90 708139 or visit www.ajsailing.com.

# The Northeast

# Getting Your Bearings

**Granite landscapes, fantastic formations of wind- and sea-sculpted rock, prehistoric stone dwellings and a beautiful, more discrete coastline scattered with islands and indented with picturesque coves – this is Gallura. The sea around here really does sparkle like a jewel and the Costa Smeralda – "Emerald Coast" – is outdazzled only by the bejewelled and glamorous people who flock to this exclusive playground.**

Planes, boats, trains and buses arrive at Ólbia, a convenient gateway to the pleasures of this beautiful region. But driving around the city can be very tedious, as it seems to be permanently under roadworks, so while it does have some good restaurants, it is not a place to linger long. From tiny Porto San Paólo, east of Ólbia, there are regular boat trips to the imposing Ísola Tavolara, standing sentinel over the bay.

The fabled Costa Smeralda is within easy reach of Ólbia, and the Pevero coastline has glorious white sandy beaches and turquoise seas. Near by are resorts such as Cannigione and Santa Teresa di Gallura, which are less glitzy but still bask along beautiful stretches of coast.

Palau is the gateway to the seven islands of the Arcipélago de La Maddalena, where a highlight is La Caprera, the home and resting place of Giuseppe Garibaldi.

The interior of the Gallura seems worlds apart from the pleasures of the beach. Arzachena is a true Sardinian town and worth visiting for its excellent prehistoric sites. The old capital of Gallura, Témpio Pausánia, is an hour's drive away through beautiful countryside up into the mountains. You will come across lakes and waterfall walks on the way up to the highest peak, Monte Limbara.

In this region of great contrasts, it is a delight to discover yet another side of Sardinia.

**Page 117: Villa roof tiles, Porto Cervo**

**Left: Palau on the Costa Smeralda at sunset**

# ★ Don't Miss

Santa Teresa di Gallura **7**
Capo Testa
133bis

Parco Nazionale dell' Arcipélago de La Maddalena **4**
Ísola Maddalena
La Maddalena □
**6** Ísola Caprera
Compendio Garibaldino di Caprera
133 □ Palau

Vignola Mare l'Agnata □
Basscutena □
125
**5** Porto Cervo

Arzachena **8**
Cannigione □
**3** Punta Capaccia
Costa Smeralda
Porto Rotondo □
Golfo Aranci □
Capo Figari

765 133
Serra di lu Tassu
Lago di Liscia
427

Ággius & Valle della Luna **10**
Lúras □
Calangiánus □
427
Monti Ultana
ílici
127
**9** Témpio Pausánia
1359 ▲ Punta Balestrieri
127
127
125
Ólbia **1**
Golfo di Ólbia
Ísola Tavolara **2**
Riserva Marina
Ísola Molara
Capo Coda Cavallo

392
Lago del Coghínas
Berchidda
199
Monti di Alà
389
□ Monti
199
E840
1316cn
199
597
□ Oschiri
389
□ Padru

1077 ▲ Punta di Senalonga
926 ▲ Punta sa Mesa
□ Alà dei Sardi
Altopiano di Buddusò

1093 ▲ Monte Lerno
Pattada □
Lago Lerna
□ Budduso

0 ——— 20 km
0 ——— 10 miles

# At Your Leisure

# In Four Days

If you're not quite sure where to begin your travels, this itinerary
recommends a practical and enjoyable four days exploring the
northeast of Sardinia, taking in some of the best places to see using
the Getting Your Bearings map on the previous page.
For more information see the main entries.

## Day 1

### Morning
Arrive in ❶ Ólbia (right; ➤ 122).
Walk up to the old part of
town and the Corso Umberto.
Take a look at the Basilica di
San Simplicio (past the level
crossing and railway station),
then make your way to Porto
San Paólo to take a boat trip to
Ísola Tavolara.

### Lunch
Eat at Ristorante da Tonino on
Ísola Tavolara (➤ 133), then
spend the afternoon relaxing on
the beach.

### Afternoon
Return to Ólbia and, if time permits,
travel to Cannigione to stay overnight.
Enjoy dinner here, perhaps at
L'Ancora (➤ 133), and make a visit
to the night market, which is open
during the summer season.

## Day 2

### Morning
Set off for the ❸ Costa Smeralda
(➤ 124–125), and make your way
to Porto Cervo. Admire the boats in
the marina or do a spot of top-end
window shopping in the ❺ Piazzetta
(left; ➤ 128).

### Lunch
Explore the beaches and have lunch
in Cala di Volpe at the very reasonably
priced Bar Baretto Pizzeria, which
serves really good pizzas and salads
on an outdoor terrace.

**Afternoon**
Take a boat trip or relax on the beaches. Stay overnight in either in Palau or in Santa Teresa.

# Day 3

**Morning**
Set off to visit the **4 Arcipélago de La Maddalena** (➤ 126–127). There are regular ferries from Palau, which you can take as a foot passenger or with a car. Enjoy a stroll around the old town of La Maddalena and have a coffee in the Piazza Garibaldi and/or take a boat trip to the islands of the archipelago and have lunch on board.

**Afternoon**
Enjoy exploring the other islands, including Caprera (accessible also by road), perhaps with a visit to **6 Compendio Garibaldino di Caprera** (➤ 128), Garibaldi's home and museum. Return to the mainland.

# Day 4

**Morning**
Set off for inland Gallura and head to **8 Arzachena** (➤ 129–130). Take a look at Il Fungo rock and then visit Coddu Vecchiu and the nearby Tomba dei Giganti di Li Lolghi (below) and Necropoli di Li Muri. From here make your way to **9 Témpio Pausánia** (➤ 130).

**Lunch**
There are pleasant restaurants to choose from in Témpio Pausánia.

**Afternoon**
West of Témpio, the hillside village of **10 Ággius** (➤ 130) is a good place to visit for its handicrafts and Museo Etnográfico. Out of town to the north is the lunarscape of the **10 Valle della Luna** (➤ 130). Return to the coast.

# ⓘ Ólbia

Ólbia's origins were Phoenician before the town became a Roman trading post, and today it is Sardinia's busiest passenger port. Few vestiges of its former glory remain but the Basilica di San Simplicio is Gallura's most important medieval church.

On arrival at Ólbia, which is one of the island's main entry points by ferry or air, you could be forgiven for trying to get out of it as quickly as possible – it is busy, traffic-choked and full of roadworks. However, the cobbled lanes in the old part of town around **Corso Umberto** are full of good restaurants and pretty piazzas to linger in over a drink. From here, past the railway station, you come to the town's top sight, the **Basilica di San Simplicio**. This 11th to 12th century Pisan Romanesque church is hewn out of Galluran granite. Inside there are columns and other pieces of masonry salvaged from Phoenician and Roman temples. In the apse there are two 13th-century frescoes, the left-hand one of which depicts San Simplicio, the patron saint of Ólbia. His feast day on 15 May brings the city's biggest celebration, lasting for three days and centred around the old church.

A café in Piazza Margherita, Ólbia

Fortunately for those who don't want to linger here, Ólbia has good bus connections from the airport and the ferry terminal and, from the city centre, to Cágliari and other cities by train and to all parts of the Costa Smeralda by bus.

### TAKING A BREAK

Enjoy the street life at one of the many **outdoor cafés** or restaurants along Corso Umberto.

✚ 161 D3

# 2 Ísola Tavolara

The giant Tavolara rock, more than 564m (1,850 feet) high, towers over the bay of this tiny island just to the south of Ólbia. Part of a protected marine park and a favourite with peregrine falcons, the island is one of the smallest kingdoms on the planet.

**Porto San Paolo, Tavolara**

The eastern side of Tavolara is a military zone, but there's free access to the inhabited western side, which even has a cemetery. Here are the **tombs of Tavolara's kings**, as Tavolara, despite its size, is a kingdom.

When King Carlo Alberto of Sardinia visited the island in 1833 for a spot of goat hunting and feasting, he thanked his host, Giuseppe Bertoleoni, by "crowning" him an independent sovereign monarch. Since then the island's "kings" have all descended from the Bertoleoni family; the present sovereign, Carlo II, runs Ristorante da Tonino (➤ 133). Wild goats still roam and it is a paradise for birds, including eagles and peregrine falcons. On the southern tip there's a good beach at **Spalmatore di Terra.**

Evidence of human occupation during the Paleolithic age has been found on the island, which in that era was connected to the mainland. About 10,000 years ago the causeway connecting it eroded into the sea.

**Boat rides** to the island are easy to find in the little beach town of Porto San Paolo, which also offers the nearest overnight accommodation, and several restaurants. Also on the mainland, at the southern point of the extensive Tavolara Marine Reserve, San Teodoro is surrounded by beautiful white sand beaches.

Tavolara island hosts an **open-air film festival** of non-mainstream Italian films, which are screened on the beach, in mid-July for four or five nights. For more information contact the Ólbia tourist office or visit www.cinematavolara.it.

# 3 Costa Smeralda

The waters of the Emerald Coast sparkle like a precious jewel,
reflected in the diamonds and platinum of those who flock
to this millionaires' playground. In the 1950s the Aga Khan
fell in love with the sandy beaches and idyllic coves along
this 10km (6-mile) coastal strip and made it an exclusive
resort. But the charms of this coastline are not confined to the
"Smeralda"; gorgeous beaches and bays are all around.

The Costa Smeralda begins around 12km (7.5 miles) north of
Ólbia and extends just 10km (6 miles) between the Golfo di
Cugnana and Golfo di Arzachena, but has a beautiful 56km
(35-mile) coastline. The area has stuck firmly by the guiding
principle that all development should blend into the **superb
scenery** without disfiguring it in any way. So there are no
high-rise buildings; telephone wires and electrical cables have
to be hidden underground; and the buildings are a curious
mix of Aegean island, contemporary and Moroccan styles.

## Porto Cervo
Porto Cervo is the only real town and "capital" of the area.
Imitating a Mediterranean fishing village, it's a pleasant place
to stroll, to see and be seen – and to window shop (► 128).
It all tends to be very quiet during the day as everyone is
relaxing on their boat, in a villa or on the beach. The best time
to visit is at sunset and later.

## Other Resorts
The Pevero coastline that has made Sardinia so famous is
lined with beaches and coves accessed by rough tracks off the
road leading to Porto Cervo. West of the Cala di Volpe bay,
Capriccioli and Romazzino beaches are good stopping points.
   On the eastern side of the Golfo di Cugnana is **Porto
Rotondo**. It is a chichi resort with obligatory marina, and is
the site of Silvio Berlusconi's 40-room Villa La Certosa. Not
really part of the Costa Smeralda, as it was developed later,

**A café terrace
in Porto Cervo**

this coast also has beautiful beaches and is equally expensive to stay in.

To the south, the resort of **Golfo Aranci** lies on the tip of Capo Figari. This is more of a family resort, with lovely beaches helpfully numbered from one to five – the third of which, "La Terza Spiaggia", is the best.

Also within easy reach of Costa Smeralda is **Cannigione** on the Gulf of Arzachena – an attractive, lively village with a picturesque port and marina. You can still sport your Prada shades but you're not so likely to go over your credit limit here. The nearby headland, **Capo d'Orso**, is a huge, bear-shaped rock. It is 122m (400 feet) high and affords stunning views across to Corsica and the Maddalena islands.

### TAKING A BREAK

**The popular white sandy beach of Báia Sardinia**

**L'Ancora** at La Conia (➤ 133), just north of town in the hills, serves everything from pasta to seafood.

➕ 161 E4

## COSTA SMERALDA: INSIDE INFO

**Top tips** The Porto Cervo marina hosts **many regattas and races**, including the Settimana delle Bocche at the end of August, the Sardegna Cup for yachts and the Premio Offshore for powerboats.

■ Borrow or rent a boat to reach all those **hideaway coves and beaches**.

**Hidden gem** The lovely beach **Portu Li Coggi** (or Spiaggia del Principe, the Prince's Beach), is poorly signposted, but is really worth a little effort. From Cala di Volpe, keep the famous hotel to the right while heading south for about 2.5km (1.5 miles). Before Capriccioli take the junction for Romazzino on the left. Head north and near the resort (1.4km/800m) take a right towards the sea. After about 300m (330 yards) downhill you come to a barrier preventing car access. From here a short mule track takes you to the shore.

# ④ Arcipélago de La Maddalena

Seven dreamy islands with Caribbean-blue seas make up the archipelago north of the Costa Smeralda. The only developed island is La Maddalena itself, from where there is a causeway to Garibaldi's island, La Caprera. But there are boat trips to see the other islands, including Spargi and Budelli with its glorious pale pink beach, Spiaggia Rosa.

Rocks hewn over thousands of years characterize the landscape of the Gallura, and on La Maddalena there are about 150 of them whose shapes have earned them nicknames such as Rabbit Rock, Eagle's Beak, De Gaulle, Dinosaur, and even Il Mostro di Lochness (Loch Ness Monster).

### La Maddalena Town
The most popular way of getting to La Maddalena is by the 20-minute ferry crossing from Palau to La Maddalena town. This is a bustling place with cobbled streets and piazzas, and a decorous *passeggiata* along the Via Garibaldi, the main street connecting Piazza Umberto I to Piazza Garibaldi. There are also some good restaurants around the squares and pleasant bars in which to people-watch.

**Boats in the harbour of La Maddalena town**

There are few sights, but the **Museo Diocesano** has some fascinating exhibits, including gifts from Lord Horatio Nelson. The Commander of the British fleet made regular visits here aboard *Victory* from 1803 to 1805 to keep an eye on the French fleet anchored in the port of Toulon. He struck up a good relationship with Agostino Millelire, Commander of the Port of La Maddalena, and on his departure, presented two silver candlesticks and a crucifix to the church, **Chiesa di Santa Maria Maddalena**. Proudly displayed in the museum with the silver "treasures" is Nelson's letter of 18 October 1804 thanking the inhabitants for their treatment of his fleet. There is also a huge display of *ex voto* gifts, including 500 rings, ranging from the very poor to the very, very rich.

Out of the centre on the road to Cala Spalmatore (about 1km/0.6 miles) you come to the **Museo Archeológico Navale** on Via Panoramica. The main exhibits are of a Roman cargo ship that was wrecked in the waters of the archipelago around 120BC, showing a reconstructed cross-section of the hull and amphorae, most of which contained wine.

## La Caprera

To the east of the island a causeway links to pine-covered La Caprera. As well as visiting the Garibaldi museum (➤ 128), this is a pleasant place to walk or cycle around (➤ 147–148).

## Beaches

The best beaches on La Maddalena are Cala Maiore Spiaggia di Bassa Trinità and Stagno Torto on the west coast and Cala Lunga in the northeast.

On Caprera there are the Due Mari beaches in the south and, in the east, Cala Brigantino and Cala Colticcio. The other islands are reachable only by boat.

**TAKING A BREAK**

Have a drink or snack at La Maddalena's **Osteria Enoteca da Liò**, Corso Vittorio Emanuele 2/6 (tel: 0789 737507).

➕ 161 D5 🚢 Regular ferries from Palau, and from Cannigione and Santa Teresa in season

**A cyclist on the causeway linking La Maddalena to La Caprera**

### Museo Diocesano
✉ Chiesa di S Maria Maddalena, Via Baron Manno 📞 078 973 7400 🕐 Tue–Sun 10–1, 3–8

### Museo Archeológico Navale
✉ Via Panoramica 📞 078 979 0660 🕐 May–Sep Tue–Sun 10:30–12:30, 3:30–7; Oct–Apr 10:30–12:30

## ARCIPÉLAGO DE LA MADDALENA: INSIDE INFO

**In more depth** The archipelago was declared a **national park** in 1996. Controversially, the US Navy established a nuclear submarine base on Ísola Santo Stefano in 1973, during the Cold War. The base was closed in 2008, dealing a locally lamented blow to the region's economy.

■ The islands were known to the Romans as Cuniculariae – "rabbit islands", and rabbits still hop about and wild boar roam. You will see signs everywhere exhorting you not to feed the boars *(vietato dar da mangiare ai cinghiali)*.

# At Your Leisure

### 5 Porto Cervo's Piazzetta

The Piazzetta is full of cool archways, loggias, bars and shops. Members of the international jet set rub shoulders with tourists and there are numerous designer boutiques to drool over. All the usual suspects are here, including Bulgari, Dolce & Gabbana and Valentino, where a pair of shoes will set you back €1,000 at a conservative estimate. Overlooking the Piazzetta is the Cervo Hotel, whose piano bar and terrace are a favourite gathering place and a gorgeous spot to indulge in a sundowner. Try a *fragolino*, a delicious *aperitivo* of strawberries with vodka and sparkling wine.

➕ 161 D4

### 6 Compendio Garibaldino di Caprera

Revered even in his own lifetime as the father of the Italian nation, Giuseppe Garibaldi (1807–82) made La Caprera his home in 1855. It was his refuge after his campaigns in the pursuit of unification, and he found solace in the peace and wild nature of this island.

In the courtyard stands a majestic pine planted by Garibaldi on the day his daughter Celia was born (he had seven children by three wives and one by a governess).

Compendio Garibaldino di Caprera

The house, Casa Bianca, has changed little since his death. His personal effects include his trademark red shirt (*camicia rossa*), after which his troops – the Red Shirts – were named, and two embroidered fez hats. The rooms are small and simple, with the exception of his death chamber. Built at the request of his wife, Francesca, it looks out to the Straits of Bonifacio and towards Nice, the city of his birth. In this room a calendar shows the date of his death, 2 June 1882. His tomb in the garden is made of rough granite, in contrast to the elaborate marble tombs of five of his children and his last wife.

➕ 161 D5  ✉ Compendio Garibaldino di Caprera  🕐 Tue–Sat 9–1:30, 2–6:30, Sun 9–1:30  💶 Moderate

### 7 Santa Teresa di Gallura

Lying on the northernmost tip of the island, this is now a very popular summer resort. From the main Piazza Vittorio Emanuele, the Via del Mare leads to the 16th-century Spanish watchtower, Torre di Langosardo.

Shops line Piazza Vittorio Emanuele in Santa Teresa di Gallura

**Roccia Il Fungo (Mushroom Rock) is on Via Limbara in Arzachena**

From here you can drink in the glorious views over the Strait of Bonifacio to Corsica. A path leads west of the tower to the main beach, Spiaggia Rena Bianca. Ferries leave daily for the 50-minute trip across to Bonifacio on Corsica – a great day out for a French lunch and some shopping. There are also boat trips to the Maddalena islands.

The granite headland, Capo Testa, lies 4km (2.5 miles) to the west. It has two beaches: the one on the left-hand side has crystalline waters and soft sand that shelves gently, while the beach on the right has amazing rock formations.

The town is a favourite of sailors, who test their skills in some of Europe's most challenging waters in the Strait of Bonifacio. Its varying winds and currents make sailing especially exciting.

🚗 160 B5

**Torre di Longosardo**
🕐 Jun–Sep daily 10–12:30, 4–7
💶 Inexpensive

## ⑧ Arzachena Prehistoric Sites

Away from the coast, discover giants' tombs and megalithic stone circles in the prehistoric remains dotted in the woods and fields around Arzachena, about half an hour's drive from Ólbia. Among olive groves, myrtle and prickly pear, the Nuraghe Albucciu, 2km (1 mile) southeast of the town, is one of Gallura's best-preserved *nuraghi*. It has an unusual granite roof that is flat rather than conical. About 4km (2.5 miles) south of Arzachena is Coddu Vecchiu, one of the island's most complete "giants' tombs". The original corridor tomb is estimated to date to the 18th to 16th centuries BC, before it was extended in Nuraghic times by adding a forecourt edged by stone.

Close by are the Tomba dei Giganti di Li Lolghi and Necropoli di Li Muri. Li Lolghi rises on a hillock and, although similar to Coddu Vecchiu, is nearly twice as long in the inner chamber. The necropolis of Li Muri is reached by returning on the rough track to the left fork going west off the track from the road signposted Luogosanto. This burial site is estimated to date back to 3500BC and consists of several rectangular tombs of stone slabs encircled by smaller slabs. There are five central circles that contained bodies buried

A craggy mountain in the lunar landscape known as Valle della Luna

in a crouching position. Beside each tomb there are standing stones, some of which have fallen over, and small stone boxes. Note that except for visiting the Nuraghe, entrance gates are usually left open when ticket kiosks are closed.

Although it makes a useful base, the town of Arzachena itself doesn't merit a long visit; the most interesting thing to see is the natural rock sculpture Roccia Il Fungo (Mushroom Rock) at the end of Via Limbara.
➕ 161 D4

**Nuraghe Albucciu**
🕐 Jul–Sep daily 9–8; Easter–Jun, Oct 9–1, 3–7
💶 Inexpensive

**Coddu Vecchiu**
🕐 Jul–Sep daily 9–8; Easter–Jun, Oct 9–1, 3–7
💶 Inexpensive

**Tomba dei Giganti di Li Lolghi and Necropoli di Li Muri**
☎ 340 8209749  🕐 Easter–Oct daily 9–7;
Nov–Easter phone for times  💶 Inexpensive

## 9 Témpio Pausánia

Témpio Pausánia, in the heart of the Gallura, lies at 550m (1,820 feet) surrounded by dense forests of cork oak. This granite hilltop town, joint capital of the province of Ólbia-Témpio, is a centre of cork manufacturing and wine production, especially Vermentino. It is a town of

churches, the most important of which is the 15th-century Cattedrale di San Pietro, substantially rebuilt in the 19th century. Next door, the Oratorio del Rosario, built by the Aragonese and rebuilt in the 18th century, has an elaborate baroque altar decorated with pure gold. A walking path climbs through the pines from a series of cascading stone fountains at Fonte Nuova, to a park surrounding hilltop mineral springs.
➕ 160 B3

## 🔟 Ággius and Valle della Luna

Lying 10km (6 miles) west of Témpio, the hill village Ággius is famous for its handicrafts, especially woven carpets (➤ 29), which are still made by hand and sold at an exhibition centre. The Museo Etnográfico gives a fascinating insight into this craft and traditions of inland Gallura. The narrow streets of this hillside town climb between houses built of the local granite, and at the top a sign directs you to the dramatic Valle della Luna (Valley of the Moon) – a lunar landscape where enormous granite rocks rise out of the ground in fantastic, contorted shapes.
➕ 160 B3

**Museo Etnográfico**
✉ Via Monti di Lizu  ☎ 079 621029;
www.aggius.net  🕐 Mid-May to mid-Oct daily
10–1, 4–8:30; mid-Oct to mid-May Tue–Sun
10–1, 3:30–7

# Where to...
## Stay

**Prices**

Expect to pay per double room, per night

€ under €90     €€ €90–€155     €€€ €155–€250     €€€€ over €250

## OLBIA

### Hotel Cavour €–€€

This small hotel with 21 rooms is in the centre of Olbia's old town. Tastefully refurbished, it is mostly cool white with pastel shades. There is a pleasant outdoor terrace, where breakfast is served in summer, and on-site parking.

➕ **161 D3** ☒ **Via Cavour 22** 🕾 **078 920 4033; www.cavourhotel.it**

### Hotel Centrale €€

This very central is clean and welcoming, with plenty of marble and minimalist lines, the rooms are pleasant and comfortable and have air conditioning and WiFi. Stays are on a bed-and-breakfast basis only.

➕ **161 D3** ☒ **Corso Umberto 85** 🕾 **078 923017; www.hotel-olbia.it**

### Hotel Gallura €€

This small, family-run hotel, near both the train and bus stations, is pleasingly decorated in traditional Sardinian style. All of the 16 rooms are air conditioned and have satellite televisions. The acclaimed restaurant (▶ 133) serves excellent breakfasts as well as other meals.

➕ **161 D3** ☒ **Corso Umberto 145** 🕾 **078 92464**

## COSTA SMERALDA

### Hotel Abi d'Oru €€€–€€€€

Lying on the Marinella Gulf, 6km (3.5 miles) from Porto Rotondo, this salmon-coloured resort-style hotel is located on a beautiful bay. The rooms are comfortable, uncluttered and of a good size and most enjoy sea views. In the grounds there is a large freshwater swimming pool, a lake that attracts birdlife and chanting frogs, and paths leading down to the white sandy beach. There are two bars and two restaurants and a pizzeria on the beach. Facilities include a children's club and tennis courts.

➕ **161 E4** ☒ **Golfo di Marinella, Porto Rotondo** 🕾 **078 930 9019; www.hotelabidoru.it** 🕲 **Apr–Oct**

### Hotel Baja €€€

This four-star property is just 200m (220 yards) from the seafront. Designed by a French architect, the interior is a vision in white and minimalist in style. The 61 rooms are spacious and comfortable, and there's a penthouse suite with an outdoor terrace and Jacuzzi/hot tub. The restaurant is good, the outdoor swimming pool inviting, and the large, fully equipped spa with complete wellness and fitness centre caters for all your health and beauty needs.

➕ **161 D4** ☒ **Via Nazionale, Cannigione** 🕾 **078 989 2041; www.clubhotelbajasardinia.it** 🕲 **Apr–Sep**

### Cala di Volpe €€€€

The glitziest of all the Starwood group properties, this is a fantasy of Moroccan-inspired architecture originally designed by French architects Michele Busiri and Jacques Couelle. Planned to replicate a fishing village, it has its own private port and jetty jutting out into the eponymous bay. The decor is rustic, with rough plaster walls and older-style furniture, but the refurbished bathrooms are decorated with Sardinian marble and handmade ceramics. The clientele is rich and famous and the poolside buffets are legendary for their celebrity-spotting opportunities. There is a seawater swimming pool, nine-hole putting green, sauna and fitness centre.

➕ 161 D4 ✉ Porto Cervo ☎ 078 997 6111; www.starwoodhotels.com 🅲 Mar–Oct

## Cervo Hotel €€€€

The most "villagey" of all the Starwood hotels, this is right in the heart of Porto Cervo in the piazzetta, with views over the marina. There are two wings – the Tennis Club, which has 16 rooms, and the Cervo Wing, with the more expensive rooms. The rustic rooms have an understated elegance, and most have their own terrace or balcony with views over the harbour, pool or *piazzetta*. There are five stylish restaurants in and around the hotel, and the exclusive designer boutiques and bars are just a glance away.

➕ 161 D4 ✉ Piazzetta, Porto Cervo ☎ 078 993 1111; www.sheraton.com

## Hotel Pitrizza €€€€

Small and über-chic, this villa-style hotel is the perfect hideaway for couples. It is also the most expensive of the five-star hotels on the Costa Smeralda. It is understated yet very sophisticated, with its own private beach and an infinity pool. The decor is traditional Sardinian and all 55 rooms are elegant. The Pitrizza Restaurant and Grill next to the pool has splendid views over the sea, and the Pitrizza bar has a spacious terrace.

➕ 161 D4 ✉ Porto Cervo ☎ 078 993 0111; www.starwoodhotels.com 🅲 May–Sep

## Hotel Romazzino €€€€

This five-star, set in flower-filled gardens with its own beach, is built in typical Sardinian style, with curved, whitewashed walls. Inside it is furnished in local natural materials, and rooms have balconies or terraces. Well suited for families, it has a playground, children's club and dining and babysitting. Along

with a seawater swimming pool, it offers tennis, water sports and a fitness centre.

➕ 161 D4 ✉ Porto Cervo ☎ 078 997 7111; www.starwoodhotels.com 🅲 Apr–Oct

## SANTA TERESA DI GALLURA

## Marinaro €€

This pleasant peach-coloured three-star hotel is in the centre of the town in a quiet street, but close to the beach. Inside, green and white stripes are the signature colours, and the airy bedrooms have been tastefully refurbished. Rooms have balconies and there are lovely views from the top floor. There is also a good restaurant. It is family run with charming, helpful staff.

➕ 160 B5 ✉ Via Angioy 48 ☎ 078 975 4112; www.hotelmarinaro.it

## ARZACHENA

## Tenuta Pilastru €–€€

Just being able to stroll to dinner at this country inn's outstanding

restaurant (▶ 134) is enough reason to choose it. The setting below wind-sculpted rocks in a landscape of spectacular mountain vistas, and the individual bungalows with hand-crafted details make it the perfect antidote for the excesses of the nearby Costa Smeralda. It's a good base for exploring the Maddelena islands and their beaches, or just to savour the scenery and quiet from your private terrace.

➕ 161 D4 ✉ Località Pilastru (on the road to Bassacutena) ☎ 078 982936; www.tenutapilastru.it

## AGGIUS

## Agriturismo Il Muto di Gallura €€

Bungalows with contemporary furnishings join the granite farmhouse in this rural retreat that includes stables of Arabian horses for guests to ride.

➕ 160 B3 ✉ Località Fraiga ☎ 079 620559; www.mutodigallura.com

# Where to...
## Eat and Drink

### Prices

Expect to pay per person for a meal, excluding drinks, tax and tip:

€ under €26     €€ €26–€55     €€€ over €55

## ÓLBIA

### Da Antonio €

Good fixed-price menus and pizzas are served in this stone-clad trattoria in the centre of Ólbia.

➕ 161 D3 ⊠ Via Garibaldi 48 ☎ 078 960 9082

### Ristorante Gallura €€

This very popular restaurant serves a blend of creative and traditional Gallurese dishes in elegant rustic surroundings. Specials include *anemoni di mare fritti* (fried sea urchins), rabbit in saffron and mussels. You must reserve ahead.

➕ 161 D3 ⊠ Corso Umberto 145 ☎ 078 924648 ⏰ Tue–Sun

## ISOLA DI TAVOLARA

### Ristorante da Tonino €€

Tonino's is run by the present-day "king" of Tavolara (his coat of arms decorates the restaurant). There is an enticing veranda on the beach and the speciality is fish and seafood, served with great aplomb. Bar service includes sandwiches and snacks.

➕ 161 D3 ⊠ Via Tavolara 14 ☎ 078 958570 ⏰ Summer Wed–Mon lunch and dinner

## COSTA SMERALDA

### L'Ancora €€

About 1km (0.6 miles) north of Cannigione, is this deservedly popular restaurant. Focaccia bread smeared with olive oil and rosemary or pecorino cheese is offered as a complimentary starter. *Antipasti* include smoked tuna and lobster, the woodburning oven makes delicious fresh pizzas and there's an excellent range of meat dishes.

➕ 161 D4 ⊠ Località La Conia, Cannigione ☎ 078 986086; www.lancoraristorante.it ⏰ Daily lunch and dinner

### Antonella & Gigi Ristorante-Pizzeria €€

This rustic, family-run restaurant is very good value for the location, serving simply prepared classics such as *insalata di mare* (seafood salad), *prosciutto e melone* (melon and ham) and a "catch of the day".

➕ 161 E4 ⊠ Villaggio Juniperus, Porto Rotondo ☎ 078 934238 ⏰ Wed–Mon 12–3, 7–11

### Mama Latina €€

This pizzeria/restaurant is one of the few open year-round. Given the pricey surroundings, this is a reasonable option with inexpensive pizzas in the front café and good salads and fish dishes in the stylish dining room.

➕ 161 D4 ⊠ Porto Cervo Marina ☎ 078 991312 ⏰ Apr–Sep daily lunch and dinner; Oct–Mar Mon–Sat lunch and dinner

### Tanit €€€

This is the place to go if you want to push the boat out, literally, as it overlooks the very exclusive marina. A meal here makes a memorable occasion. Drinks are served on the panoramic terrace before a gourmet feast of fish and seafood specialities, although for carnivores Argentine beef also features. Service is very attentive without being fussy and prices are very high.

➕ 161 D4 ⊠ Poltu Quatu (between Báia Sardinia and Porto Cervo) ☎ 347 765 8769 ⏰ Summer daily bar from 6pm, dinner from 7

# Where to... Shop

## ARZACHENA

### Tenuta Pilastru €€

One of the island's best restaurants serves traditional Sardinian dishes elegantly, either à la carte or as a tasting menu with classic dishes from this part of the island. The surroundings match the food.

➕ 161 D4 ✉ Località Pilastru (on the road to Bassacutena) ☎ 078 982936; www.tenutapilastru.it ⏰ Daily lunch and dinner

## LA MADDALENA

### La Grotta €€

This long-established restaurant is off the Via Italia. The environment is rustic, atmospheric and bustling. Fish and seafood is piled high in dishes such as *penne alla grotta* (seafood pasta) or *aragosta sette-otto* – the signature lobster dish.

➕ 161 D5 ✉ Via Principe di Napoli 3, La Maddalena ☎ 078 973 7228; www.lagrotta.it ⏰ May–Sep daily lunch and dinner

The pretty resorts of Palau, Santa Teresa di Gallura, Baia Sardinia and Cannigione might lack the glamour and price-tag of Porto Cervo and Porto Rotondo, but many visitors will prefer their laid-back, unpretentious feel. Each has its own smattering of souvenir boutiques and night markets (the best is in Palau and stays open until 1am in the peak season).

On La Maddalena, be sure to visit **Sardegna da Mangiare e da Bere** on Piazza Garibaldi (tel: 078 973 1008), a veritable Aladdin's cave of Sardinian specialities. You will find everything here, from cheese and salamis to pasta, *dolci sardi* and wines and *mirto* liqueur, all beautifully and oh-so-temptingly displayed. You'll be lured to purchase an item or two.

# Where to... Be Entertained

## CLASSICAL MUSIC

On the Costa Smeralda, the **Chiesa di Stella Maris** in Porto Cervo has classical music concerts in the summer. Olbia has an annual summer festival, **L'Estate Olbiense**, from the end of July, with performances and concerts taking place in Piazza Margherita, as well as films and sports.

## NIGHTLIFE

The main action is a couple of kilometres south of Porto Cervo, where the trio of the Costa Smeralda's most happening clubs are on the same road.

The **Sopravento** (Località Golfo di Pevero; tel: 078 994717), **Sottovento** (Località Golfo di Pevero; tel: 078 992243) and **Billionaire Club** (Località Alto Pevero; tel: 078 994192), the latter two open only in summer.

All Costa Smeralda clubs are very exclusive, very expensive and have very strict door codes. To be admitted you need to act and dress the part and look seriously moneyed. Plenty of celebs such as Paris Hilton and P Diddy have been spotted in the flickering candlelight and secluded corners of the Moroccan-style Billionaire Club.

For lower-key entertainment and people-watching in Porto Cervo, the **Café du Port** in Porto Vecchio (tel: 078 992348) is very popular.

In Olbia the lively **Planet Café & La Movida** in Viale Aldo Moro (tel: 078 959 8559) opens its doors onto a terrace in summer.

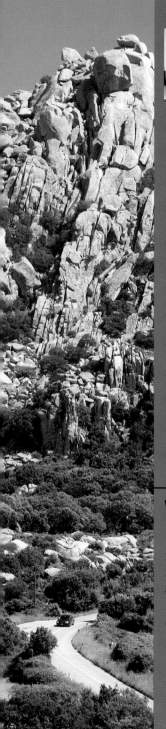

# Walks and Tours

# Cágliari

*Walk*

This walk takes you from the heart of medieval Cágliari at the Bastione San Remy, past the amphitheatre and botanic garden, down to the café-lined Via Roma.

**DISTANCE** 4km (2.5 miles) **TIME** 3–4 hours
**START POINT** Bastione San Remy ✚ 170 B4 **END POINT** Via Roma ✚ 170 B3

## 1–2

Start your walk from atop **Bastione San Remy** (▶ 46) on Piazza Costituzione. Heading north from the Bastione, walk up the Via Fossario to Piazza Palazzo, the heart of the Castello district, and you will see the **Cattedrale** (▶ 47) on your right. Look at the Pisan Romanesque-style facade and then go inside to see the baroque/Gothic decorations. The next building on your left, on the northeastern side of the Piazza Palazzo, is the **Palazzo Viceregio**, its pale green neoclassical facade contrasting with the deep rust shutters (Tue–Fri 8:30–2, 3–7, Sat 8:30–2). The reception rooms are adorned with Murano glass chandeliers, frescoed ceilings and silk-lined walls – and portraits of the Piedmontese viceroys who formerly governed Sardinia from here.

## 2–3

Continue northwards and turn right into the little Piazzetta Mercede Mundula. From here there are glorious views over the bay and convenient benches from which to admire them. Continue up the Via Pietro Martini to the Piazza Indipendenza. At the head of this piazza is the **Torre di San Pancrazio** (Tue–Sun 9–1, 3:30–7:30). Similar to the Torre dell' Elefante (▶ 47), this is one of the city's medieval constructions not to have undergone "ruinous modification", as the plaque tells you. It was built by the Pisans in 1305 and is 55m (180 feet) high; from the top there are spectacular views.

Proceed through the archway to reach the sloping Piazza Arsenale and arrive at the **Cittadella dei Musei**.

## 3–4

There are four museums here – the Pinacoteca (art gallery); the Mostra di Cere

**Remains of the Roman amphitheatre in Cágliari**

Anatomiche, a waxworks of rather gory anatomic sections; the Museo d'Arte Siamese (Southeast Asian art); and the highlight, the **Museo Archeológico Nazionale** (➤ 47).

## 4–5

After leaving the museum, turn right and go out of Porta Cristina (signposted *"ingresso al castello"*). Turn right along Viale Buon Cammino, then cross over the road with Via Anfiteatro on your left and walk under the jacaranda trees to the **Anfiteatro Romano** on your left.

At the next junction, turn left down Via Frà Ignazio da Laconi to the entrance to the Anfiteatro (Tue–Sat 9:30–1:30, Sun 10–1). Constructed out of solid rock in the second century AD, it seated 10,000 spectators (the city's entire population at the time). Although much of it has been destroyed, there is still a fascination in the former gladiatorial site.

## 5–6

Keep following the road down and turn left, remaining on Via Frà Ignazio da Laconi, to Ingresso No 11 for the **Orto Botánico** (Botanic Garden; ➤ 53). This pleasant, shady spot is the city's lungs.

## 6–7

On exit, turn left into Via Portoscalas past **Chiesa di San Michele**. Turn right onto Corso Vittorio Emanuele II, then right into Largo Carlo Felice and straight down to the **Via Roma**.

**Left: Facade of the Cattedrale di Santa Maria**

### TAKING A BREAK

**Il Caffé** at 76 Largo Carlo Felice is a good place for a drink and a browse in their very good bookshop.

---

*(Map labels)*

0 200 yards

Viale Buon Cammino

Museo Archeologico Nazionale **[4]**

Cittadella dei Musei **[3]**

Piazza Independenza

Via C T Porcell

Torre di San Pancrazio **[2]**

Palazzo Viceregio

VIALE REGINA ELENA

Cattedrale

v Fossario

Via Anfiteatro

Via Cam Nuovo

V S Margher

Via S Giorg

**CASTELLO**

Via Ospedale

Anfiteatro Romano **[5]**

*Orto Botánico*

Via Frà Ignazio da Laconi

Chiesa di San Michele **[6]**

Via Portoscalas

Via D Alberto Azuni

Piazza Yenne

CORSO VITTORIO EMANUELE II

Largo Carlo Felice

Via G Maria Angiuy

**VIA G MANNO**

Bastione San Remy

Piazza Costituzione **[1]**

**VIA ROMA** **[7]**

## 2 Cágliari to Villasímius

*Drive*

This drive takes you past the Golfo degli Ángeli (Bay of Angels) along the Strada Panorámica, which overlooks lovely beaches backed by low hills and covered with Mediterranean *macchia*. As you leave Cágliari behind, the coast becomes much quieter, the road twists and turns over hilly terrain with dramatic views of the sea, white sands and delightfully secluded coves begging to be explored.

**DISTANCE** 51km (32 miles) to Villasímius (but with detours to beaches)
**TIME** 2–3 hours or a day with all detours
**START POINT** Cágliari Airport ⊞ 168 A2 **END POINT** Villasímius ⊞ 169 D1

**The rocky shoreline between Villasímius and Cágliari**

### 1–2

Start from **Cágliari airport** (6km/3.5 miles northwest of Cágliari centre) and going southeast take the SS554, following the signs for Quartu S Elena and Villasímius (▶ 48). This is mainly dual carriageway around the ring road (and no tolls payable). As you get close to the sea, look out for flamingos in the lagoons left and right, Stagno Simbrizzi and Stagno di Quartu respectively. To reach Poetto beach (▶ 54) turn west on the coast road past Spiaggia di Quartu and on to Marina Piccola (▶ 54) on **Poetto** beach.

### 1–2 (alternative)

If you're travelling from central Cágliari (▶ 46), follow Via Roma southeast, continuing straight at the end of the harbour on the street that becomes Viale Armando Diaz. Continue by turning on to Ponto Vittorio and slightly left at Viale Poetto, then take a left turn at Via Lungo Saline.

Stop at the vast **Poetto** beach (▶ 54; it is more than 5km/3 miles long) with its fine, white sand, and admire the lagoon of Molentargius behind it, which is frequented by flamingos and many other wetland birds.

### 2–3

Continue along the panoramic Cágliari to Villasímius coastal road to the locality of **Sant' Andrea** (on the left). For a detour to the beach turn right a little further along into Via Taormina, which brings you to the shore.

On the western side there are remains of a third century AD Roman villa and thermal baths to be seen.

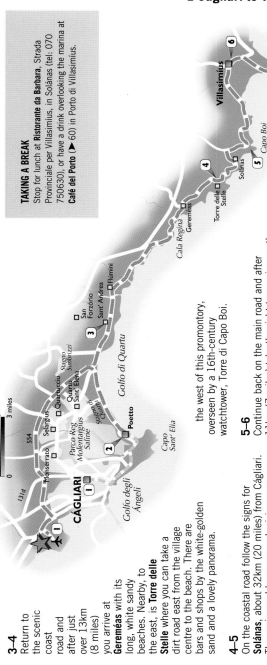

## TAKING A BREAK

Stop for lunch at **Ristorante da Barbara**, Strada Provinciale per Villasimíus, in Solánas (tel: 070 750630), or have a drink overlooking the marina at **Café del Porto** (▶ 60) in Porto di Villasimíus.

## 3–4

Return to the scenic coast road and after just over 13km (8 miles) you arrive at **Geremeás** with its long, white sandy beaches. Nearby, to the east, is **Torre delle Stelle** where you can take a dirt road east from the village centre to the beach. There are bars and shops by the white-golden sand and a lovely panorama.

the west of this promontory, overseen by a 16th-century watchtower, Torre di Capo Boi.

## 4–5

On the coastal road follow the signs for **Solánas**, about 32km (20 miles) from Cágliari. The main road loops around, giving access to the beach at the main car park, but choose the prettier, eastern side, remarkable for its dune at the base of **Capo Boi**. The large, golden sandy beach extends to

## 5–6

Continue back on the main road and after 11km (7 miles) take the right turn going south signposted **Capo Carbonara**. This is the most southeasterly point of Sardinia and from here there are excellent views. Rejoin the main road, which brings you into **Villasimíus** (▶ 48).

## Oristano and Sínis Peninsula

*Drive*

This leisurely drive takes you to the seaside resort of Marina di Torre Grande and then through the "flamingo heaven" lagoon world of Mìstras and Cábras before reaching the tip of the Sínis Peninsula at the remains of the gloriously sited ancient city of Thárros.

**DISTANCE** 49km (30 miles) **TIME** Half a day
**START/END POINT** Oristano ✚ 162 C3

### 1–2

Take the SS292 north from **Oristano** (▶ 68–69) following signs to Marina di Torre Grande and Cúglieri. A long bridge crosses the Tirso, after which you come to a fork in the road. Take the left fork, following signs for Cábras/Thárros and keep following signs for San Giovanni di Sínis. About 9km (5.5 miles) outside Oristano you come to **Marina di Torre Grande** (▶ 74). This is a buzzing seaside resort (in season) with a long, sandy beach that shelves gently and has water sports.

### 2–3

Head back to the main road and at the intersection take the left-hand turn towards

San Giovanni di Sínis. On both sides you now have lagoons. On your left is the Stagno di Mìstras, while on the right is the **Stagno di Cábras** (▶ 71), the largest in Italy at 2,000ha (5,000 acres). Besides flamingos, the lagoon also teems with fish, especially mullet, which is used to make the prized *bottarga* (mullet roe; ▶ 24–25). Go straight on, past a right turn towards Thárros, to **San Giovanni di Sínis**.

### 3–4

This sleepy fishing village's Chiesa di San Giovanni di Sínis is, after Cágliari's San Saturnino, the oldest church in Sardinia, dating from AD476. The interior is refreshingly

### View across the lagoon to the Sínis Peninsula

bare and simple. Behind the church, near the sea, are some remaining thatched *domus de cruccuri* (rush huts) once used by fishermen. Leaving the church on your left continue down the road to Thárros.

### 4–5

Founded around 730BC, **Thárros** (▶ 70) was the most prosperous of the west coast Phoenician port cities. After the Roman conquest in 238BC, however, it gradually fell into disuse as trade shifted to Oristano in 1070. The archaeological site reveals mostly

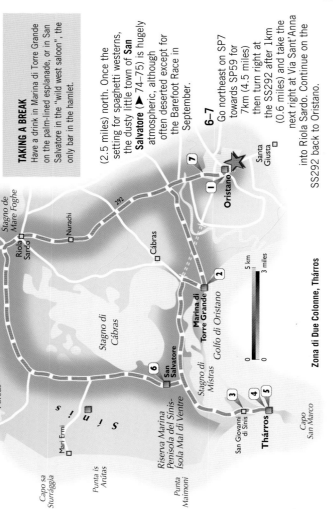

### TAKING A BREAK

Have a drink in Marina di Torre Grande on the palm-lined esplanade, or in San Salvatore in the "wild west saloon", the only bar in the hamlet.

(2.5 miles) north. Once the setting for spaghetti westerns, the dusty little town of **San Salvatore** (▶ 74–75) is hugely atmospheric, although often deserted except for the Barefoot Race in September.

### 6–7

Go northeast on SP7 towards SP59 for 7km (4.5 miles) then turn right at the SS292 after 1km (0.6 miles) and take the next right at Via Sant'Anna into Riola Sardo. Continue on the SS292 back to Oristano.

**Zona di Due Colonne, Thárros**

the Roman city, but there is still a temple with Doric half-columns and a children's burial ground (*tophet*) dating from the Phoenician city. An old watchtower stands sentinel on the headland and the coast is fringed by lovely beaches, including the nearby beach of San Giovanni di Sínis.

### 5–6

Return the same way until you reach the left turn to San Salvatore/Riola, 4km

# 4 Alghero
*Walk*

This walk takes you through the old town of Alghero (▶ 106–107), protected by ancient walls and towers. In the web of narrow streets you may pass washing hung beneath shuttered windows, and the city's most important churches and museums. The walk culminates in the main piazza, where Charles V addressed the crowds in 1541 before going off to fight the Turks.

**DISTANCE** 2km (1.2 miles) **TIME** 2–3 hours
**START POINT** Piazza Porta Terra ✚ 170 D1 **END POINT** Piazza Civica ✚ 170 B2

**1–2**
Start at **Piazza Porta Terra** (▶ 106) opposite the top end of the Giardino Púbblico. The Porta Terra was one of the walled town's two gates, and is now an interpretation centre; climb the 32 steps to the top for excellent views of the town. Coming out of here, turn left into Carrer de los Arjoles and then right into Via Ambrogion Machin. At the end of this road turn right into Via Carlo Alberto and you'll come to the **Chiesa di San Francesco** (▶ 106) on the right. This is one of Alghero's landmarks, with its stately, pointed Aragonese tower, and is an excellent example of Catalan

architecture. Parts of the cloisters date back to the 13th century. Concerts are staged in this lovely setting during the summer.

**2–3**
From the church turn left and walk back down Via Carlo Alberto. This street is Alghero's main shopping hub, full of boutiques and jewellery shops brimming with coral. Continue straight on crossing over Via Gilbert Ferret. Known as the *"quatre contonades"* (four sides), this junction was where piecemeal labourers would, over the centuries, assemble in the hope of getting work.

After this, on the left-hand side, you come to the 17th-century **Chiesa di San Michele** (▶ 106). This opulent baroque church dominates the skyline with its glistening ceramic dome, and has fine altar paintings.

**3–4**
From San Michele walk back to Via Gilbert Ferret and turn left, then right into Via

### Statues in Chiesa di San Francesco

Principe Umberto, one of the old centre's most attractive lanes. The 17th-century **Palazzo Machin** (Nos 9–11) was built for a local bishop and, although now crumbling, it

A café terrace in Piazza Civica

still has fine Catalan-Gothic windows.

Continue up the street and ahead of you, just to the right, is the cathedral's octagonal campanile. Walk around into Piazza Duomo and see the **Cattedrale di Santa Maria** (▶ 106).

Inside there is a jumble of styles and overblown baroque touches although some parts of the original 16th-century building still remain.

## 4–5

Go out of the Cattedrale and head next door to the **Museo Diocesano d'Arte Sacra**, housed in the former Rosario church. This is the perfect setting for an array of priceless religious art. Walk east past Via Maiorca, Via Carlo Alberto and Vicolo Sena to arrive at **Piazza Civica**, the old town's main square, known as "Il Salotto" (the dining room). It is just inside **Port a Mare** (Sea Gate) and is full of outdoor bars and parasols. On the opposite side of the piazza is the Gothic **Palazzo d'Albis**, from where Charles V told the assembled throng, *"Estade todos caballeros"* ("You are all knights").

### TAKING A BREAK

Rather like a pub, the **Jamaica Inn** at Via Principe Umberto 57 (www.jamaicainnalghero.com; Tue–Sun) is a good place for a snack and a drink – more wines than beers. **Il Ghiotto** (▶ 114), Piazza Civica 23, is a great place for lunch as it's a wine bar and a delicatessen.

# 5 Gennargentu Mountains

*Drive*

This scenic drive takes you through granite-strewn rolling countryside framed by lush vegetation of Mediterranean *macchia*, cork, holm and oak trees. There are tracks and gorges and majestic mountains, and vineyards around Oliena that produce some of the island's finest wines.

**DISTANCE** 77km (48 miles) **TIME** Half-day to full day
**START/END POINT** Núoro ■ 164 C4

## 1–2

Leave **Núoro** (▶ 86–87) heading east on the Via Trieste. Continue on this road, which becomes the Via Ballero, then turn left at Viale La Solitudine. After 0.3km (330 yards) bear slightly right onto the SP42, Via Monte Ortobene. Continue along this panoramic road as it twists upwards. (From Núoro the journey is about 8km/5 miles.) You will come to some speed humps on the road followed by souvenir stalls and a couple of bars/restaurants. Leave your car in the car park near the top of **Monte Ortobene** (▶ 92) and follow the faded yellow sign saying "Il Redentore". A walk of around 100m (110 yards) along a dusty track brings you to 49 rock steps up to the bronze sculpture of *Christ the Redeemer* (▶ 92).

## 2–3

The next stage, **Oliena** (▶ 92), is 12km (7.5 miles) away. Leave Monte Ortobene heading northwest on the SP42 towards the SP45/Via Valverde. Bear slightly left at SP45/Viale La Solitudine and turn left at SP45. Take a sharp left at the SS129. After 4.3km (2.7 miles) turn right at the SP22 and continue on the SP22 by turning left. Bear

**The scenery along the Núoro to Monte Ortobene road**

slightly right at Via Raffaele Calamida then turn right at Via Nuoro/SP46 and follow tourist information signs to the main Via Deledda. Here is a good place to pick up information on the area and excursions (including Tiscali ▲ 88–89 and Gola Su Gorruppu ▲ 92–93). Oliena is a very pretty town full of whitewashed houses with balconies, terraces and strange chimneypots. Perhaps taking a cue from neighbouring Orgosolo, Oliena has several wall murals, and in the parish church a Christmas *presepio* (nativity scene) by a local artist. Produced here are the excellent, fruity Cannonau wines as well as filigree silver and gold jewellery and delicately embroidered silk shawls.

### 3–4

A little diversion 6km (3.5 miles) east on the Dorgali road/SP46 takes you to **Su Gologone**, named after its spring, which rises close to the church of San Giovanni. It is also a good spot for embarking on expeditions to Tiscali and/or Gola Su Gorruppu but note that

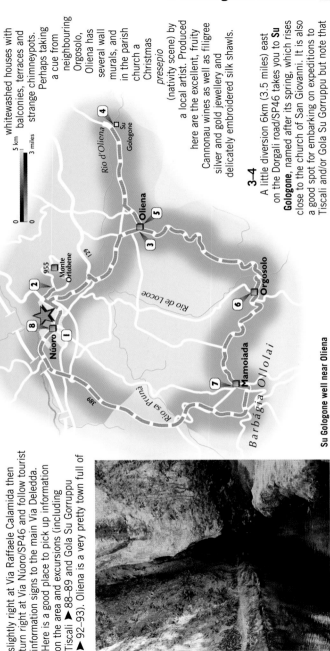

Su Gologone well near Oliena

these would take up around four hours and involve some arduous trekking. There's also a hotel, the Su Gologone, which offers many expeditions and has a good restaurant.

**4–5**
Retrace your steps on the SP46 to Oliena.

**5–6**
After about 7km (4.5 miles) outside Oliena turn left at the SP58 and follow this twisting, scenic road for about 11km (7 miles) until you see the entrance to **Orgosolo** (▲ 94). Known as the "capital of the Barbágia" and former refuge of the area's most notorious bandits, it is also famous for the murals that cover every available space depicting political themes and the locals' struggle to maintain their culture.

**6–7**
From Orgosolo head west for 10km (6 miles) to **Mamoiada** (▲ 93). Take the SP22/Corso Repúbblica towards Via di Vittorio and continue on the SP22. Famous for its masked festivals, especially at Carnival time in February/March, Mamoiada's Museo delle Mascere Mediterranee shows the famous *mamuthones* costumed figures.

The lush countryside near Monti del Gennargentu

**7–8**
From Mamoiada head southwest on Via Matteotti towards Via Núoro and turn right, then bear slightly right again at SS389/Via Vittorio Emanuele II and follow the SS389 to Núoro (16km/10 miles).

**TAKING A BREAK**
Under shady eucalyptus trees in Su Gologone is a good place to enjoy a picnic, with free-flowing therapeutic spring water. Or treat yourself to a delicious meal at the **Su Gologone restaurant/hotel** (▲ 97).

## 6 Ísola Caprera
*Walk*

**DISTANCE** 12.5km (8 miles) **TIME** 4 hours
**START/END POINT** Car park, Caprera (350m/380 yards after the causeway from La Maddalena) ⊞ 161 D5

This walk takes you through the archipelago's greenest island, known also as "Garibaldi's island". Giuseppe Garibaldi loved La Caprera's freedom and peace so much that he chose to spend the last 27 years of his life here (▶ 128). Stroll through *macchia* and past green pines enjoying stunning views over the surrounding islands and across to Corsica. The island's highest peak, pink granite Monte Telaione, reaches up to 212m (695 feet), where you may see peregrine falcons. You could also choose to take a detour to the lovely Cala Coticcio beach.

### 1–2
From the car park, take the footpath that forks right into the *macchia* going south. Follow this main path through the scented myrtle, juniper, lentisk, lavender and wild flowers, ignoring the short tracks down to the coast. After about 15 minutes you come to a grove of umbrella pine trees. Turn right at the next fork and on your right is the Cala Stagnali – a little cove with coarse sand. Keep straight on

The views from Ísola Caprera are idyllic

the main track to an asphalt road onto which you bear right. At the fork turn left and begin the ascent looking out over the archipelago's islands and Corsica. After about an hour and a quarter of walking, you'll see the peak of **Poggio Rasu** (Bare Hill) on your right. The road bends to the left but carry straight along the track to the World War II gun emplacement built from granite.

### 2–3
Return to the bend and continue right, ascending along the road. After a short distance the road begins to level out and descend. At a T-junction turn right past a derelict fountain on the left and a concrete building on the right. Continue along this road to a lay-by on the left, then after 50m (55 yards) take a little detour by turning sharp right and climb up the steps to **Monte Telaione** – Caprera's highest peak – with its lookout tower. From here you could take a detour down a steep path to the right followed by a

A blissfully quiet road on Ísola Caprera

flight of rocky steps made by the army to the little **Cala Coticcio** beach. Note that it is a very steep incline.

### 3–4

Return to the road and turn right to continue. After about 2 hours and 45 minutes (in total), shortly after you pass a derelict house on the left, follow the road as it bears left and the asphalted road runs out. On reaching a track junction, turn down to the left. (The track straight ahead leads to Monte Arbuticci's gun emplacement.) Ignore the two turns on your right and go straight ahead.

### 4–5

At a junction go left past two Military Zone buildings on the right and up to a reservoir (about 3 hours 15 minutes). Cross the wall of the dam, following the ascending path,

which eventually flattens out leading to a car park. Follow the granite drive on the right past wind-sculpted granite rocks to the **Compendio Garibaldino di Caprera** (▶ 128).

### 5–6

Before the Garibaldi buildings, take the short concrete drive on the left to a little terrace. Carry on downhill on the path below the enclosed estate until the path descends between rocks. At a small house bear right before joining a road that takes you past houses. Follow the main road left back to the small car park.

### TAKING A BREAK

Take a picnic and plenty of water to enjoy the peace of this lovely, wild island. Try to avoid weekends as locals like to drive on these tracks then.

*Ísola Budelli*

*Ísola Spargi*  *Ísola Maddalena*  La Maddalena

**Parco Nazionale dell' Arcipelago de La Maddalena**

*Ísola Santo Stéfano*  Stagnali

Palau  **Compendio Garibaldino di Caprera**  **Ísola Caprera**

Capannaccia  133  Punta Rossa

0   5 km

0   2 miles

# Practicalities

## BEFORE YOU GO

### WHAT YOU NEED

|  |  | UK | Germany | USA | Canada | Australia | Ireland | Netherlands | Spain |
|---|---|---|---|---|---|---|---|---|---|
| ● Required | Some countries require a passport to | | | | | | | | |
| ○ Suggested | remain valid for a minimum period | | | | | | | | |
| ▲ Not required | (usually at least 6 months) beyond the | | | | | | | | |
| △ Not applicable | date of entry – check before you travel. | | | | | | | | |
| Passport | | ● | ● | ● | ● | ● | ● | ● | ● |
| Visa (for less than three months) | | ▲ | ▲ | ▲ | ▲ | ▲ | ▲ | ▲ | ▲ |
| Onward or Return Ticket | | ○ | ○ | ● | ● | ● | ○ | ○ | ○ |
| Health Inoculations (tetanus and polio) | | ▲ | ▲ | ▲ | ▲ | ▲ | ▲ | ▲ | ▲ |
| Registration Document/Insurance Certificate (if own car) | | ● | ● | ● | ● | ● | ● | ● | ● |
| Travel Insurance | | ○ | ○ | ○ | ○ | ○ | ○ | ○ | ○ |
| Driving Licence (national) | | ● | ● | ● | ● | ● | ● | ● | ● |

### WHEN TO GO

**Cágliari**

High season       Low season

| JAN | FEB | MAR | APR | MAY | JUN | JUL | AUG | SEP | OCT | NOV | DEC |
|---|---|---|---|---|---|---|---|---|---|---|---|
| 10°C | 11°C | 13°C | 19°C | 22°C | 25°C | 31°C | 31°C | 26°C | 22°C | 16°C | 12°C |
| 50°F | 53°F | 55°F | 66°F | 72°F | 75°F | 88°F | 88°F | 79°F | 72°F | 61°F | 54°F |

Sun       Sunshine and showers       Wet       Cloudy

Sardinia has a very **pleasant six-month summer**, usually hot and dry from May to October but cooled by a breeze as it is the middle of the Mediterranean. In March and April evenings can be cool, but this is a **good time for walking**, when the island is covered in flowers, and there are also a number of excellent festivals. From May onwards it is usually warm enough for swimming. July and August are the **peak season** and are often swelteringly hot as well as extremely busy. September can also be very hot, but it is much less crowded. Autumn sees a second flowering of plants, while in the winter the weather can still be warm and clear with **snowfalls** in the interior, where it is possible to ski. Note that many hotels around the coast are only open from May to September. The above temperatures are the maximum daily average.

**GETTING ADVANCE INFORMATION**

**Websites**
www.sardegnaturismo.it
www.holidays-in-sardinia.
com
www.sarnow.com

**In Italy**
Italian State Tourist Board
Via Parigi 11
00185 Rome
☎ 06 488991;
www.enit.it

**In the UK**
ENIT
1 Princes Street
London W1B 2AY
☎ 020 7408 1254;
www.enit.it

## GETTING THERE

**By Air** Sardinia is served by three airports: Alghero in the northwest, Ólbia in the northeast and Cágliari in the south.

**From the UK** From London airports, easyJet flies to Cágliari and Ólbia, and Ryanair flies to Alghero and Cágliari. Other scheduled airlines operate in the summer such as BMI and British Airways, and there are many regional flights too. The flight time is 2–3 hours.

**From the US** and Canada There are no direct flights to the island, but there are flights to the mainland from several cities. The main hubs are Milan and Rome, from where there are plenty of connecting flights. The national airline, Alitalia, has the widest selection of routes between the US and Italy. Flying time to the mainland is 8–10 hours from the east coast and around 11 hours from the west coast. Connections to Sardinia take another hour or two. The most frequent flights are between Rome and Cágliari.

**From Australia and New Zealand** There are no direct flights but Air New Zealand and Qantas fly to Milan and Rome, from where it is easy to pick up a connecting flight. You could also fly to the UK first and then pick up a flight as there are so many options. Flying time to mainland Italy from Australia's east coast is 21 hours and from New Zealand is 24 hours.

**By Sea** There are several options to cross the English Channel to France and many routes from France and Italy to Sardinia: Marseille to Porto Tórres (northwest coast), Rome (Civitavecchia) to Golfo Aranci or Ólbia (northeast coast) and Genova to Porto Tórres or Ólbia, for example. There are also fast ferries from Nice to Bastia in Corsica and daily ferries from Bonifacio to Santa Teresa on the northern tip of Sardinia.

## TIME

Like mainland Italy, Sardinia is one hour ahead of GMT, although daylight saving applies from April to October, making it GMT +2.

## CURRENCY AND FOREIGN EXCHANGE

**Currency** The legal currency of Sardinia is the euro (€), which is split into 100 cents (*centésimi*). Euro notes are issued in denominations of 5, 10, 20, 50, 100, 200 and 500. There are eight different coin denominations – 1 and 2 euros, then 50, 20, 10, 5, 2 and 1 cents. All euro coins and notes are accepted in all EU member states.

**Exchange** Cash and most major travellers' cheques can be exchanged at banks and at kiosks *(cambio)* at the airports and large hotels.

**Credit and debit cards** Credit cards are widely accepted, except in B&Bs and *agriturismi*, but many smaller establishments prefer cash. Most towns have a bank with an ATM where you can use a credit or debit card, although using the former is usually expensive.

**In the US**
ENIT, 630 Fifth Avenue
Suite 1565, New York
NY 10111
☎ 212/245-5618;
www.italiantourism.com

**In Australia**
Level 4
46 Market Street
Sydney, NSW 2000
☎ 02 9262 1666;
www.enit.it

**In Canada**
175 Bloor St East
Suite 907, South Tower
Toronto, ON, M4W 3R8
☎ 416/925 4882;
www.italiantourism.com

## WHEN YOU ARE THERE

### NATIONAL HOLIDAYS

| | |
|---|---|
| 1 Jan | New Year's Day |
| 6 Jan | Epiphany |
| Mar/Apr | Good Friday and Easter Monday |
| 25 Apr | Liberation Day |
| 1 May | Labour Day |
| 2 Jun | Republic Day |
| 15 Aug | Ferragosto (Assumption) |
| 1 Nov | Ognissanti (All Saints) |
| 8 Dec | Immaculate Conception |
| 25 Dec | Christmas Day |
| 26 Dec | St Stephen's Day |

Each region also observes an Anniversary Holiday.

### ELECTRICITY

The current is 220 volts AC. However, appliances requiring 240 volts AC also work. Plugs are standard two-round-pin continental types. UK, North American and Australasian visitors will need an adaptor, and US visitors will need a voltage transformer.

### OPENING HOURS

○ Shops
● Offices
● Banks
● Post Offices
● Museums/Monuments
● Pharmacies

8am 9am 10am noon 1pm 2pm 4pm 5pm 7pm

☐ Day  ☐ Midday  ☐ Evening

Some shops close Monday morning and most shops are closed on Sunday. Museum times vary but are usually daily 9–1, 4–8 (3–7 in winter). Some museums close on Monday. Archaeological sites usually open from 9 to one hour before sunset. Smaller museums and places of interest have limited opening during winter and some close down completely.

### TIPS/GRATUITIES

Small tips are often expected. As a general guide:

| | |
|---|---|
| Restaurants (service included) | Change |
| Restaurants (service not included) | 10% |
| Cafés/bars (if service not included) | Change or 10% |
| Taxis | Discretionary |
| Tour guides | Discretionary |
| Porters | €1–€2 |
| Chambermaids | Discretionary |
| Hairdressers | 10% |
| Toilets | Discretionary |

### KNOCK-OFF NO-NO

No matter how cute that Louis Vuitton knock-off may be, resist the temptation to buy it, especially from beach vendors. Italian police have recently begun a crack-down on illegally "branded" goods, fining the buyers as much as €1,000. Although there have been no reports in Sardinia yet, it's safer to stay out of illegal trade altogether.

### TIME DIFFERENCES

| GMT | Sardinia | Netherlands | USA (West Coast) | USA (New York) | Australia (Sydney) |
|---|---|---|---|---|---|
| 12 noon | 1pm | 1pm | 4am | 7am | 10pm |

## STAYING IN TOUCH

**Post** The postal service is very slow. You can buy stamps *(francobolli)* at post offices, tobacconists *(tabacchi)* and some souvenir shops. Post offices are normally open Mon–Fri 8:10–6:50, Sat 8–1:15.

**Public telephones** Telecom Italia (TI) payphones can be found on streets and in bars and some restaurants. Usually you need a phonecard *(scheda telefónica)*, available in €3, €5 or €10 denominations and sold at newsstands or *tabacchi*. Tear the perforated corner off before use.

Phone tariffs are very expensive – among the highest in Europe. To get through to an English-speaking operator, dial 170.

| International Dialling Codes | Dial 00 followed by |
|---|---|
| UK: | 44 |
| USA / Canada: | 1 |
| Irish Republic: | 353 |
| Australia: | 61 |
| Germany: | 49 |

**Mobile providers and services** Signals are quite good in most places. Be sure your provider allows you roving access to other networks. Mobiles work on the GSM European standard; visitors from North America can buy compatible SIM cards at phone and electronics shops in Cágliari and larger cities. Check your own provider's rates before travelling; it may be cheaper to make international or other calls from a land line.

**WiFi and Internet** All larger hotels and even many small ones now offer some type of Internet. Larger ones have WiFi in rooms and most provide it in at least some public area. There is often a charge (about €10 for 24 hours) for in-room use. Signal strength and connection speed varies greatly and you may need to take your laptop to the lobby even if there is supposedly in-room connectivity. WiFi is available in many cafés and most towns have an internet point; ask at the tourist office.

## PERSONAL SAFETY

The bandits that once roved the mountains are long gone, and Sardinia is one of Italy's safest regions. However, in larger cities such as Cágliari it makes sense to take the usual precautions – petty theft related to drug addiction is on the increase.
To be safe:
- Close bags and wear them in front, across your body.
- Leave valuables and jewellery in the hotel safe.
- Never leave luggage or other possessions visible in parked cars.
- Wear your camera and don't leave it unattended in cafés and restaurants.
- Avoid parks and beaches late at night.
- Because beaches are crowded in summer, they are especially tempting places for petty thieves (who are very likely not locals themselves). Don't leave anything on a lounger or towel that you can't afford to lose – especially your mobile.

**Police assistance:**
📞 112 from any phone

**EMERGENCY NUMBERS**

**POLICE 112**

**FIRE 115 (OR 113)**

**AMBULANCE 118 (OR 113)**

**GENERAL EMERGENCY 113**

## HEALTH

 **Insurance** You should always take out full travel insurance cover when visiting Sardinia. EU citizens can reclaim medical expenses if they travel with their European Health Insurance Card (EHIC). There are reciprocal arrangements between the Australian Medicare system and Italy, but comprehensive insurance is still advised.

 **Doctors and Dentists** Ask at a pharmacy or your hotel for details of English-speaking doctors. Common ailments include dehydration, sunburn, stomach upsets and mosquito bites. Use insect repellent and sun protection. Dental treatment is not covered by the health service and can be expensive – another reason to carry medical insurance.

 **Weather** The sun is at its hottest in July and August, with temperatures frequently over 30°C (86°F), but it's always possible to cool off in the sea or mountains. Two summer winds sweep across the island – the *maestrale* (mistral) from the northwest, and the sultry, sand-bearing sirocco from the south. You should take a sun hat, high-factor suncream and plenty of water to drink.

 **Drugs** Prescriptions and other medicines are available from pharmacies *(farmacie)*, indicated by a large green cross.

 **Safe Water** Tap water is generally safe to drink and is free in bars, although many people choose bottled water. Sardinia has many mountain springs from which you can drink. *"Acqua non potabile"* indicates non-drinking water.

## CONCESSIONS

**Students/Youths** An International Student Identity Card (ISIC) entitles holders to discounts (usually half the normal fee) at museums and archaeological sites. There are three *ostelli per la gioventù* (youth hostels) on the island, which offer inexpensive accommodation; see www.ostellionline.org
**Senior Citizens** Admission to some sites is reduced for those aged 65 (sometimes 60) or over.

## TRAVELLING WITH A DISABILITY

The national museums in Cágliari have dedicated ramps, lifts and lavatories, but otherwise wheelchair access is extremely limited. Prehistoric sites and monuments generally have very difficult access, and the same is true of medieval city centres, which often have cobbled streets. Hotels at the more luxurious end are generally well equipped.

## CHILDREN

Children are welcomed with open arms in Sardinia. Many resorts have crèches (day-care) and children's clubs. The sun can be fierce so it is essential to provide adequate protection against sunburn and dehydration.

## TOILETS

There are few public toilets on the island. Most bars have them (*bagno, gabinetto* or *toilette*) and most are relatively clean, although it's always a good idea to carry some toilet tissue with you.

## CUSTOMS

The import of wildlife souvenirs from rare or endangered species may be illegal or require a permit. Before buying, check your home country's regulations.

## EMBASSIES AND HIGH COMMISSIONS

|  | | |  |  |
|---|---|---|---|---|
| **UK** | **USA** | **Ireland** | **Australia** | **Canada** |
| ☎ (070) 828628 (Cágliari) | ☎ (06) 46741 (Rome) | ☎ (06) 697 9121 (Rome) | ☎ (06) 852721 (Rome) | ☎ (06) 85444 2911 (Rome) |

## USEFUL WORDS AND PHRASES

The official language of Sardinia is Italian, and most Sardinians speak it clearly. The Sardinian language is a melting pot of many influences – around Alghero you will hear Catalan, for example – but if there is one language from which Sardo takes its root it is Latin, and it is closer to this mother tongue than mainland Italian is; for example, Sard for house is *domus* rather than Italian *casa*. The other major difference is the replacement of the Italian definite articles il, la, i and le with su, sa, sus, sos and sas, similar to Catalan. People appreciate you greeting them with a *buon giorno* or *buona sera*. *Grazie* (thank you) should be acknowledged with *Prego* (You're welcome). *Permesso?* (May I?) is the polite way of making your way through a crowded street.

## SURVIVAL PHRASES

yes/no **sì/non**
please **per favore**
Thank you **Grazie**
You're welcome **Di niente/Prego**
I'm sorry **Mi dispiace**
Goodbye **Arrivederci**
Good morning **Buongiorno**
Goodnight **Buona sera**
How are you? **Come sta?**
How much? **Quanto costa?**
I would like... **Vorrei...**
Open **Aperto**
Closed **Chiuso**
Today **Oggi**
Tomorrow **Domani**
Monday **Lunedì**
Tuesday **Martedì**
Wednesday **Mercoledì**
Thursday **Giovedì**
Friday **Venerdì**
Saturday **Sabato**
Sunday **Domenica**

## DIRECTIONS

I'm lost **Mi sono perso/a**
Where is...? **Dove si trova...?**
the station **la stazione**
the telephone **il telefono**
the bank **la banca**
the toilet **il bagno**
Turn left **Volti a sinistra**
Turn right **Volti a destra**
Go straight on **Vada dritto**
At the corner **All'angolo**
the street **la strada**
the building **il palazzo**
the traffic light **il semaforo**

the crossroads **l'incrocio**
the signs for... **le indicazione per...**

## IF YOU NEED HELP

Help! **Aiuto!**
Could you help me, please? **Mi potrebbe aiutare?**
Do you speak English? **Parla inglese?**
I don't understand **Non capisco**
Please could you call a doctor quickly? **Mi chiami presto un medico, per favore**

## RESTAURANT

I'd like to book a table **Vorrei prenotare un tavolo**
A table for two, please **Un tavolo per due, per favore**
Could we see the menu, please? **Ci porta la lista, per favore?**
What's this? **Cosa è questo?**
A bottle of/a glass of... **Un bottiglia di/un bicchiere di...**
Could I have the bill? **Ci porta il conto**

## ACCOMMODATION

Do you have a single/double room? **Ha una camera singola/doppia?**
with/without bath/toilet/shower **con/senza vasca/gabinetto/doccia**
Does that include breakfast? **E'inclusa la prima colazione?**
Does that include dinner? **E'inclusa la cena?**
Do you have room service? **C'è il servizio in camera?**
Could I see the room? **E' possibile vedere la camera?**

## MENU READER

**Sardinian
specialities:**
**bottargo** mullet roe
**bue rosso** prized
Sardinian beef
**cavallo** horse
**cordula** lamb tripe
**culurgiones** ravioli
filled with potato
and cheese
**mallareddus** small
pasta
**porceddu** roast
suckling pig
**sebada** baked
pastry filled with
cheese and honey
**suspiros** sweets
made with almonds,
eggs and lemon
**zuppa Gallura** hearty
baked dish of bread,
cheese and broth
**zurrette** black
pudding

**Other menu items:**
**acciuga** anchovy
**acqua** water
**affettati** sliced cured
meats
**affumicato** smoked
**aglio** garlic
**agnello** lamb
**anatra** duck
**antipasti** hors
d'oeuvres
**arista** roast pork
**arrosto** roast
**asparagi**
asparagus
**birra** beer
**bistecca** steak
**bollito** boiled meat
**braciola** minute
steak
**brasato** braised
**brodo** broth
**budino** pudding
**burro** butter

**cacciagione** game
**cacciatore, alla** rich
tomato sauce with
mushrooms
**caffè corretto/
macchiato** coffee
with liqueur/spirit, or
with a drop of milk
**caffè freddo** iced
coffee
**caffè latte** milky
coffee
**caffè lungo** weak
coffee
**caffè ristretto**
strong coffee
**calamaro** squid
**cappero** caper
**carciofo** artichoke
**carne** meat
**carota** carrot
**carpa** carp
**casalingo** home-
made
**cavolfiore**
cauliflower
**cavolo** cabbage
**ceci** chickpeas
**cervello** brains
**cervo** venison
**cetriolino** gherkin
**cetriolo** cucumber
**cicoria** chicory
**cinghiale** boar
**cioccolata**
chocolate
**cipolla** onion
**coda di bue** oxtail
**coniglio** rabbit
**contorni**
vegetables
**coperto** cover
charge
**coscia** leg of meat
**cotolette** cutlets
**cozze** mussels
**crema** custard
**crudo** raw
**dolci** cakes/
desserts

**erbe aromatiche**
herbs
**facito** stuffed
**fagioli** beans
**fagiolini** green beans
**fegato** liver
**finocchio** fennel
**formaggio** cheese
**forno, al** baked
**frittata** omelette
**fritto** fried
**frizzante** fizzy
**frulatto** whisked
**frutti di mare**
seafood
**funghi** mushrooms
**gamberetto** shrimp
**gelato** icecream
**ghiaccio** ice
**gnocchi** potato
dumplings
**granchio** crab
**gran(o)turco** corn
**griglia, alla** grilled
**imbottito** stuffed
**insalata** salad
**IVA** VAT
**latte** milk
**lepre** hare
**lumache** snails
**manzo** beef
**merluzzo** cod
**miele** honey
**minestra** soup
**molluschi** shellfish
**olio** oil
**oliva** olive
**ostrica** oyster
**pancetta** bacon
**pane** bread
**panino** roll
**panna** cream
**pastasciutta** dried
pasta with sauce
**pasta sfoglia** puff-
pastry
**patate fritte** chips
**pecora** mutton
**pecorino**
sheep'smilk cheese

**peperone** red/ green
pepper
**pesce** fish
**petto** breast
**piccione** pigeon
**piselli** peas
**pollame** fowl
**pollo** chicken
**polpetta** meatball
**prezzemolo** parsley
**primo piatto** first
course
**ragù** meat sauce
**ripieno** stuffed
**riso** rice
**salsiccia** sausage
**saltimbocca** veal
with prosciutto
andsage
**secco** dry
**secondo piatto** main
course
**senape** mustard
**servizio compreso**
service included
**sogliola** sole
**succa di frutta** fruit
juice
**sugo** sauce
**tonno** tuna
**uovo affrogato/in
carnica** poached egg
**uovo al tegamo/
fritto** fried egg
**uovo alla coque** soft
boiled egg
**uovo alla sodo** hard
boiled egg
**uova strapazzate**
scambled egg
**verdure** vegetables
**vino** wine
  **bianco** white
  **rosato** rosé
  **rosso** red
**vitello** veal
**zucchero** sugar
**zucchino**
courgette
**zuppa** soup

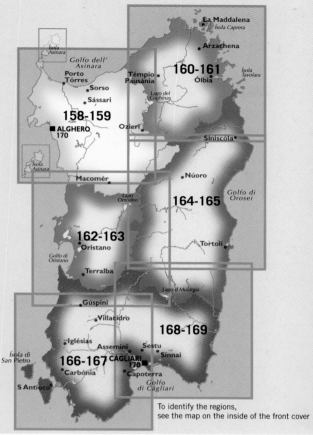

La Maddalena
*Isola Caprera*

Arzachena

**160-161**

*Isola Tavolara*

Porto
Tórres
Tempio
Pausánia
Olbia

Sorso
*Golfo dell'
Asinara*

*Isola
Asinara*

Sássari

*Lago del
Coghinas*

**158-159**

Ozieri

Siniscóla

ALGHERO
170

*Isola
Asinara*

Macomér

Núoro

*Golfo di
Orosei*

*Lago
Omodeo*

**164-165**

**162-163**

Oristano

Tortolí

*Golfo di
Oristano*

Terralba

*Lago d'Mulárgia*

Gúspini

Villacidro

**168-169**

Iglésias

Sestu

Assemini

CÁGLIARI

Sinnai

*Ísola di
San Pietro*

**166-167**

170

Carbónia

Capoterra

*Golfo
di Cágliari*

S Antíoco

To identify the regions,
see the map on the inside of the front cover

## Regional Maps

- ═══ Major route
- ═══ National road
- ─── Regional/other/minor road
- ┄┄┄ Railway
- ┈┈┈ Restricted area
- ☐ City
- ▫ Town/village
- ✈ Airport
- ▣ Featured place of interest
- ▪ Place of interest

**158-169** | 0 ——— 10 km
0 ——— 5 miles

## Streetplans

- ═══ Main/other/minor road
- ─── Railway/city wall
- ▨ Important building
- ▨ Park/garden
- ▣ Featured place of interest
- *i* Tourist information
- † Church
- ✉ Post Office

**170**
**Cágliari** | 0 ——— 400 metres
0 ——— 400 yards

**170**
**Alghero** | 0 ——— 150 metres
0 ——— 150 yards

# Atlas

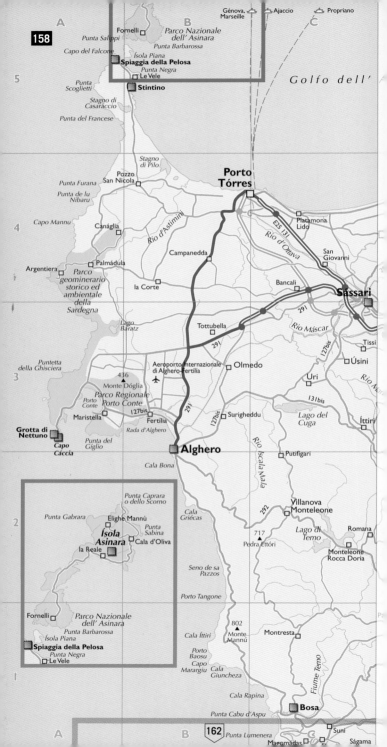

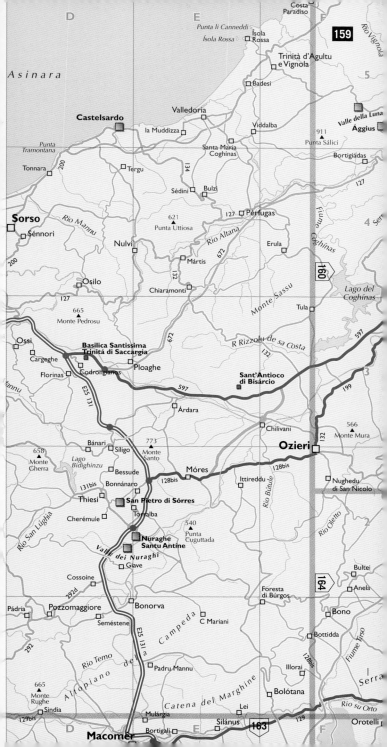

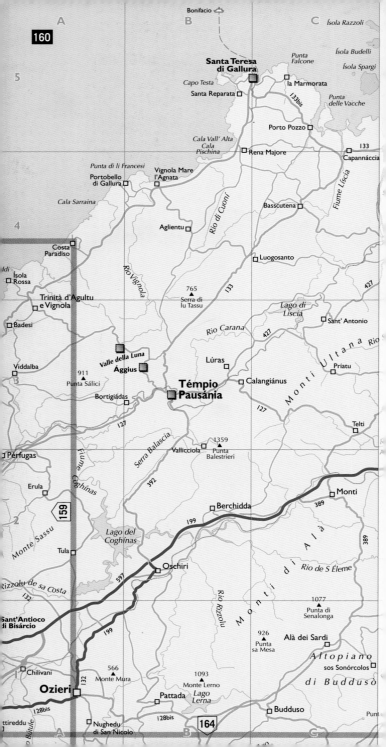

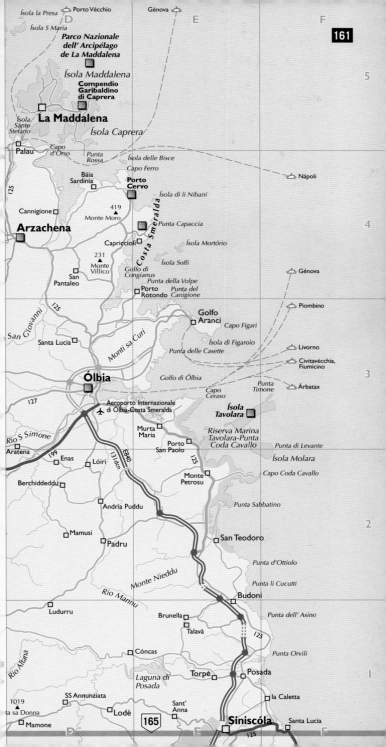

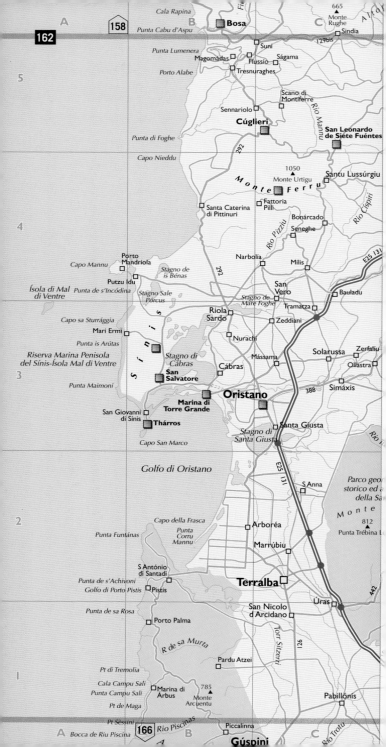

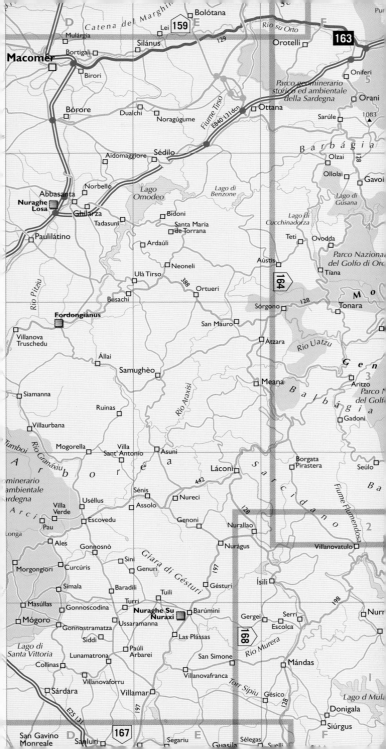

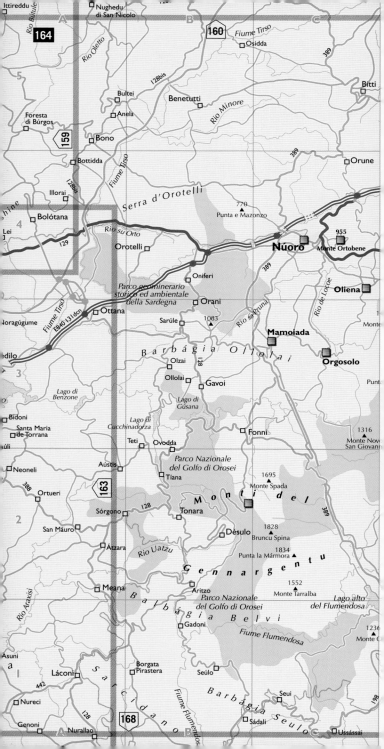

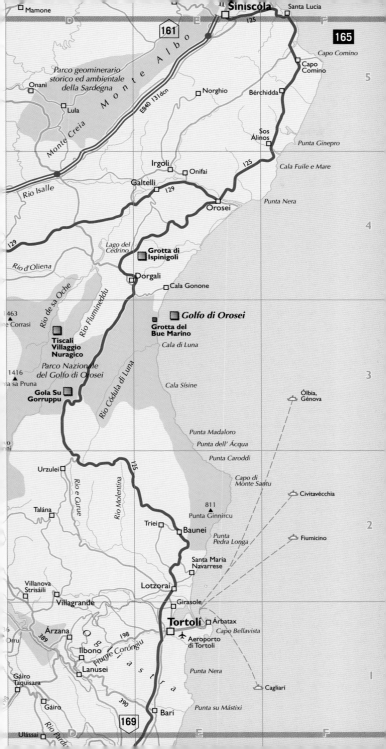

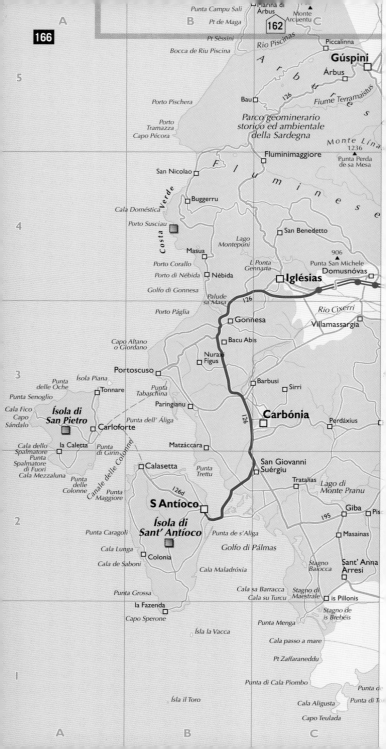

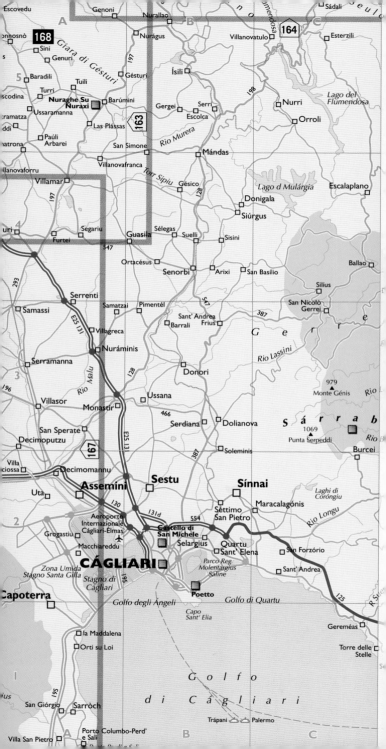

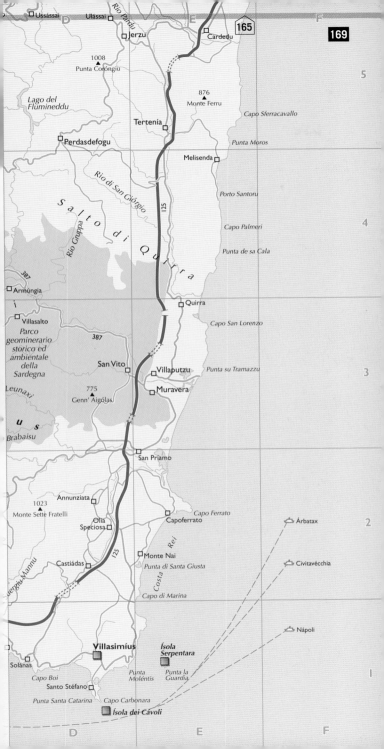

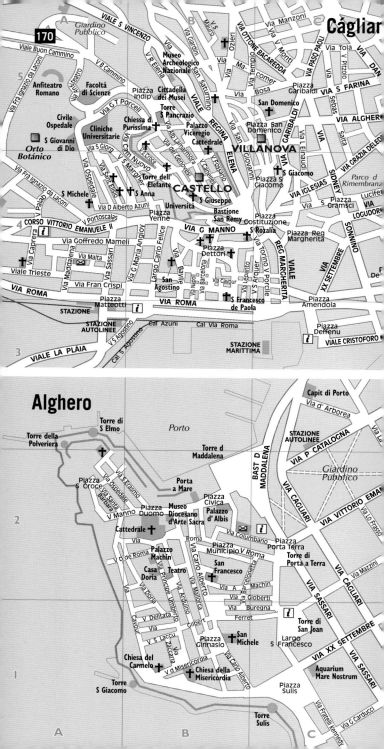

## Picture credits

The Automobile Association wishes to thank the following photographers and organisations for their assistance in the preparation of this book.

Abbreviations for the picture credits are as follows – (t) top; (b) bottom; (l) left; (r) right; (c) centre; (AA) AA World Travel Library

**2i** MORANDI Bruno/ Hemis/ Photolibrary.com; **2ii** AA/ Neil Setchfield; **2iii** Alexander Pöschel/ imagebroker.net/ Photolibrary.com; **2iv** AA/ Neil Setchfield; **2v** © MARKA / Alamy; **3i** © Bartek Wrzesniowski / Alamy; **3ii** AA/ Clive Sawyer; **3iii** AA/ Neil Setchfield; **5l** MORANDI Bruno/ Hemis/ Photolibrary.com; **5c** AA/ Clive Sawyer; **5r** AA/ Neil Setchfield; **6-7** Stillman Rogers Photography © 2009, 2010; **8** AA/ Neil Setchfield; **9tl** AA/ Neil Setchfield; **9bl** AA/ Neil Setchfield; **9r** AA/ Neil Setchfield; **10-11** AA/ Neil Setchfield; **12l** AA/ Neil Setchfield; **12r** AA/ Neil Setchfield; **13l** Joerg Reuther/ imagebroker.net/ Photolibrary.com; **13r** AA/ Neil Setchfield; **14-15** © claudio h. artman / Alamy; **15** INSET © Cubolmages srl / Alamy; **16** © David Sutherland / Alamy; **17t** Bruno Morandi / Robert Harding; **17b** © Cubolmages srl / Alamy; **18** AA/ Neil Setchfield; **19** AA/ Neil Setchfield; **20** AA; **21** AA/ Neil Setchfield; **22l** Stillman Rogers Photography © 2009,2010; **22r** Stillman Rogers Photography © 2009,2010; **23** JIRI JIRI/ Mauritius/ Photolibrary.com; **24t** © Cubolmages srl / Alamy; **24c** AA/ Neil Setchfield; **24b** Stillman Rogers Photography © 2009,2010; **26-27** ImageBroker/FLPA; **27l** Panda Photo/FLPA; **27r** AA/ Neil Setchfield; **28- 29t** © John Ferro Sims / Alamy; **28l** Carlo Rebecchi / SUBERIS; **28r** AA/ Neil Setchfield; **29l** The Art Archive / Archaeological Museum Cagliari / Gianni Dagli Orti; **29r** AA/ Neil Setchfield; **30t** © John Ferro Sims / Alamy; **30b** © Cubolmages srl / Alamy; **31l** AA/ Neil Setchfield; **31c** AA/ Neil Setchfield; **31r** AA/ Neil Setchfield; **41l** Alexander Pöschel/ imagebroker.net/ Photolibrary.com; **41c** AA/ Neil Setchfield; **41r** AA/ Neil Setchfield; **44t** AA/ Neil Setchfield; **44b** AA/ Neil Setchfield; **45** AA/ Neil Setchfield; **46-47** Doug Pearson/ Jon Arnold Travel/ Photolibrary.com; **47** AA/ Neil Setchfield; **48** AA/ Neil Setchfield; **49** AA/ Neil Setchfield; **50** AA/ Neil Setchfield; **51** AA/ Neil Setchfield; **52** AA/ Neil Setchfield; **53** AA/ Neil Setchfield; **54t** SIME/Spila Riccardo/4Corners Images; **54b** AA/ Neil Setchfield; **55** AA/ Neil Setchfield; **56** AA/ Neil Setchfield; **57t** Bruno Morandi/ Robert Harding; **57b** Stillman Rogers Photography © 2009, 2010; **63l** AA/ Neil Setchfield; **63c** AA/ Neil Setchfield; **63r** AA/ Neil Setchfield; **64** AA/ Neil Setchfield; **66** AA/ Neil Setchfield; **67t** AA/ Neil Setchfield; **67b** Sheila Terry/ Robert Harding; **68-69** AA/ Neil Setchfield; **70** AA/ Neil Setchfield; **71** © Cubolmages srl / Alamy; **72** Oliviero Olivieri/ Robert Harding; **73** AA/ Neil Setchfield; **74** Dallas Stribley/ Lonely Planet Images; **75t** AA/ Neil Setchfield; **75b** AA/ Neil Setchfield; **76** AA/ Neil Setchfield; **81l** © MARKA / Alamy; **81c** AA/ Neil Setchfield; **81r** AA/ Neil Setchfield; **82** AA/ Neil Setchfield; **84** AA/ Neil Setchfield; **85t** AA/ Neil Setchfield; **85b** AA/ Clive Sawyer; **86t** AA/ Neil Setchfield; **86b** © MARKA / Alamy; **87** AA/ Neil Setchfield; **88** AA/ Neil Setchfield; **89** © Cubolmages srl / Alamy; **90-91** AA/ Neil Setchfield; **91** AA/ Neil Setchfield; **92** © Neil Setchfield / Alamy; **93** AA/ Neil Setchfield; **94** AA/ Neil Setchfield; **99l** © Bartek Wrzesniowski / Alamy; **99c** AA/ Neil Setchfield; **99r** © Vincent MacNamara / Alamy; **100** AA/ Neil Setchfield; **102** © Travelwide / Alamy; **103t** © Jon Arnold Images Ltd / Alamy; **103b** Bruno Manunza/ Tips Italia/ Photolibrary.com; **104** AA/ Neil Setchfield; **105** AA/ Neil Setchfield; **106** AA/ Neil Setchfield; **107** AA/ Neil Setchfield; **108** AA/ Neil Setchfield; **109** AA/ Neil Setchfield; **110** AA/ Neil Setchfield; **111** AA/ Neil Setchfield; **112** AA/ Neil Setchfield; **117l** AA/ Clive Sawyer; **117c** © Jon Arnold Images Ltd / Alamy; **117r** © Cubolmages srl / Alamy; **118** © claudio h. artman / Alamy; **119** © Gregory Preest / Alamy; **120t** AA/ Neil Setchfield; **120b** © travelstock44 / Alamy; **121** AA/ Neil Setchfield; **122** AA/ Neil Setchfield; **123** © Cubolmages srl / Alamy; **124** AA/ Neil Setchfield; **125** AA/ Neil Setchfield; **126** AA/ Neil Setchfield; **127** AA/ Neil Setchfield; **128t** AA/ Neil Setchfield; **128b** AA/ Neil Setchfield; **129** AA/ Neil Setchfield; **130** AA/ Neil Setchfield; **135l** AA/ Neil Setchfield; **135c** AA/ Neil Setchfield; **135r** AA/ Neil Setchfield; **136** AA/ Neil Setchfield; **137** AA/ Neil Setchfield; **138** AA/ Neil Setchfield; **140** AA/ Neil Setchfield; **141** AA/ Neil Setchfield; **142** AA/ Neil Setchfield; **143** AA/ Neil Setchfield; **144** AA/ Neil Setchfield; **145** © imagebroker / Alamy; **146** AA/ Neil Setchfield; **147** AA/ Neil Setchfield; **148** AA/ Neil Setchfield; **149l** © Cubolmages srl / Alamy; **149c** AA/ Neil Setchfield; **149r** AA/ Neil Setchfield; **153t** AA/ Neil Setchfield; **153c** AA/ Neil Setchfield; **153b** AA/ Neil Setchfield

Every effort has been made to trace the copyright holders, and we apologise in advance for any accidental errors. We would be happy to apply any corrections in the following edition of this publication.

# **SPIRAL**GUIDE
# Questionnaire

## Dear Traveller

**Your comments, opinions and recommendations are very important to us. Please help us to improve our travel guides by taking a few minutes to complete this simple questionnaire.**

You do not need a stamp (unless posted outside the UK). If you do not want to remove this page from your guide, then photocopy it or write your answers on a plain sheet of paper.

Send to: The Editor, Spiral Guides, AA World Travel Guides, FREEPOST SCE 4598, Basingstoke RG21 4GY.

## Your recommendations...
We always encourage readers' recommendations for restaurants, night-life or shopping – if your recommendation is used in the next edition of the guide, we will send you a FREE AA Spiral Guide of your choice. Please state below the establishment name, location and your reasons for recommending it.

_____

_____

_____

_____

_____

**Please send me AA Spiral** _____
(see list of titles inside the back cover)

## About this guide...
**Which title did you buy?**

_____ **AA Spiral**

**Where did you buy it?** _____

**When?** m m / y y

**Why did you choose an AA Spiral Guide?** _____

_____

_____

_____

**Did this guide meet your expectations?**

Exceeded ☐   Met all ☐   Met most ☐   Fell below ☐

**Please give your reasons** _____

_____

_____

_____

_____

continued on next page...

**Were there any aspects of this guide that you particularly liked?**

---

**Is there anything we could have done better?**

---

## About you...

Name (Mr/Mrs/Ms)

Address

Postcode

Daytime tel no _____ email _____

Please *only* give us your email address and mobile phone number if you wish to hear from us about other products and services from the AA and partners by email or text or mms.

**Which age group are you in?**

Under 25 ☐   25–34 ☐   35–44 ☐   45–54 ☐   55–64 ☐   65+ ☐

**How many trips do you make a year?**

Less than one ☐   One ☐   Two ☐   Three or more ☐

Are you an AA member? Yes ☐   No ☐

---

About your trip...

When did you book? m m / y y        When did you travel? m m / y y

How long did you stay?

Was it for business or leisure?

Did you buy any other travel guides for your trip?   ☐ Yes  ☐ No

If yes, which ones?

---

**Thank you for taking the time to complete this questionnaire. Please send it to us as soon as possible, and remember, you do not need a stamp (unless posted outside the UK).**